LEADVILLE

by Dave Southworth

Front and back cover design by Chip Southworth

Library of Congress Cataloging-In-Publication Data

Southworth, Dave,
Leadville

      Bibliography: p.
      Includes index.

1.Colorado—History—Biography. 2. Mining Camps—Colorado—History. 3. Lawmen—Colorado—Biography. 4. West (U.S.)—History—Biography. 5. Outlaws—West (U.S.)—Biography. 6. Lawmen—West (U.S.)—Biography. 7. West (U.S.)—History—Sources. 8. Frontier and Pioneer Life—West (U.S.)—Sources.

ISBN: 978-1-890778-09-5
      1-890778-09-5

Copyright: 2010 by Dave Southworth

All rights reserved. Without limiting the rights under copyright reserved above, no part of this book may be reproduced, stored in or introduced into a retrieval system, or transmitted, in any form or by any means (electronic, mechanical, photocopying, recording or otherwise) without the written permission of the copyright owner.

Contents

Introduction	Page 7
Lake County Map	Page 10
Leadville Area Map	Page 11
Gold, Silver, and the Growth of a City	Page 13
Augusta and Horace Tabor	Page 21
Baby Doe and the Tabor Triangle	Page 31
They Made Their Mark	Page 41
Leadville Color	Page 45
Toughs and Tarts	Page 49
The Suburbs	Page 61
Legends of Lost Gold	Page 69
The Firefighters	Page 73
Cloud City Society	Page 75
The Iron Horse	Page 79
Labor Disputes	Page 83
J.J. and the Unsinkable Mrs. Brown	Page 85
The Great Ice Palace	Page 89
Climax Molybdenum	Page 91
Glossary of Mining Terms	Page 95
Bibliography	Page 101
Index	Page 105

Introduction

By the time our nation was founded, in 1776, it was obvious that western expansion was inevitable. Much wide open, unexplored country lay west of the Mississippi River. Spain claimed a large part of this territory, but there was uncertainty over the exact location of the boundary lines. In 1806, the United States government dispatched a military man, Zebulon Montgomery Pike, to explore this vast area in an effort to find the river boundary between the United States and Spanish territories. As his expedition crossed part of what is now Colorado, the explorers viewed a huge mountain on the horizon. They traveled for days in an effort to reach the mountain, but it seemed to get no closer. As snow and freezing temperatures set in, Pike had to abandon his trek. Zebulon Pike never climbed the mountain, nor did he name it for himself, but the landmark became known as "Pikes Peak."

Lewis Ralston and his group of southern prospectors discovered gold at Ralston Creek, near its confluence with Clear Creek, during the summer of 1850. This find, near present day Arvada, is generally considered Colorado's first authenticated gold discovery. It didn't amount to much, however, so Ralston and his men pushed on toward the gold fields of northern California.

In 1858, William Green Russell, and his party from Georgia discovered gold at Dry Creek. With their picks and shovels, hundreds of prospectors flocked to the camps of Denver City and Auraria. The cry was "Pikes Peak or Bust!" After ravaging the stream beds, however, with little to show for it, most left in disgust calling the strike a hoax. They were premature in their decision, for two major gold strikes occurred during the following spring. Discoveries by George Jackson near present day Idaho Springs and John Gregory near present day Central City brought thousands more stampeding into the territory. By the summer of 1859, over 5,000 men were working the Gregory Lode with more than 100 sluices.

Famed New York newspaper man Horace Greeley, awed by all the commotion, decided he should see for himself and traveled to Mountain City (adjacent to present day Central City). Although the miners were unimpressed with Greeley's lecture against drinking and gambling, he was conversely impressed with their discoveries. He declared, "...the news of your rich discovery shall go forth all over the world." And it did. As his articles circulated, people came from all over America and many countries abroad.

These discoveries enticed prospectors to push deeper into the mountains in search of gold deposits. Pioneers headed west taking with them their hopes, memories, and whatever they could stuff into their wagons. Denver emerged as a supply town for the mining camps. The first gold discovery near present day Leadville occurred the following spring, while that area was still a part of Kansas Territory. In February of 1861, Colorado Territory was established.

Mining camps originally popped up as tent cities. Tents were soon replaced by log cabins constructed of squared-hewn timber. As sawmills were built, frame structures were constructed, often with tall and massive false fronts. Stores were often erected shoulder-to-shoulder so the imposing fronts could hide the buildings behind them. When a town showed signs of permanence, some stone and brick buildings were erected. Finer homes were often built of Victorian architecture. Some of those in Leadville were trimmed with elaborate gingerbread.

The earliest mining camps had sanitation problems. Trash was often thrown into the streets. Animals contributed to the refuse. Personal cleanliness was minimal. Miners worked up a sweat during the daytime, then often slept in their clothes because tent walls were thin and mountain nights were chilly. Many never bothered to bathe, especially during colder weather. As a result, epidemics were common. Men outnumbered women in the early camps by a margin of 30 to 1. As more women and more families arrived in later migrations, cleanliness improved and camps became more comfortable.

Placer mining was most common in the early 1860s. Prospectors scrambled up and down the streams in search of color. When successful, they staked their claims and panned the stream beds. Others combed the mountains in search of exposed ore or float gold. When the easily obtainable gold disappeared, miners tunneled into the mountain sides, sinking shafts to reach their veins. Gold found in this manner was difficult to extract from the ore. Smelters soon solved the ore reduction problem.

The presidential election of 1876 was a primary catalyst toward Colorado obtaining statehood. While Republican Ulysses S. Grant's second term as President was drawing to a close, the Republican candidate, Rutherford B. Hayes, was locked in a hotly contested battle with the Democratic nominee, Samuel Tilden. The Colorado Territory was predominantly Republican. If granted statehood, it could contribute three electoral votes to Hayes, so President Grant proclaimed Colorado a state on August 1, 1876. The declaration was strategic because Rutherford B. Hayes defeated Samuel Tilden by one electoral vote, to become the nineteenth President of the United States. Because it was admitted to the union during the nation's centennial year, Colorado was dubbed the "Centennial State."

During the '70s and '80s mining really boomed. When silver was discovered in Leadville in 1877, the population of Lake County grew to nearly 24,000. In a few short months, silver became more dominant than gold throughout the state.

The population explosion was abetted by a maze of railroads which snaked through valleys and over mountains bringing supplies and more people. The railroads also provided a means of shipping ore from the mines to the smelters with a lot less hardship.

Leadville sits at an elevation of 10,152 feet amidst some of the loftiest mountains in North America. The Sawatch (Blue Earth) Range lies to the west, with Mount Elbert, Colorado's highest peak, and Mount Massive. The Mosquito Range extends from north to south, east of the city. There was a time when Mosquito Pass saw much traffic to and from the towns of Buckskin Joe, Alma and Fairplay.

The early history of Leadville is as interesting and colorful as any mining town in the West. The Cloud City, as it is known, has its own special story – a story that has become legendary because of its myriad of extraordinary inhabitants. There were colorful characters of all kinds – and this is their story.

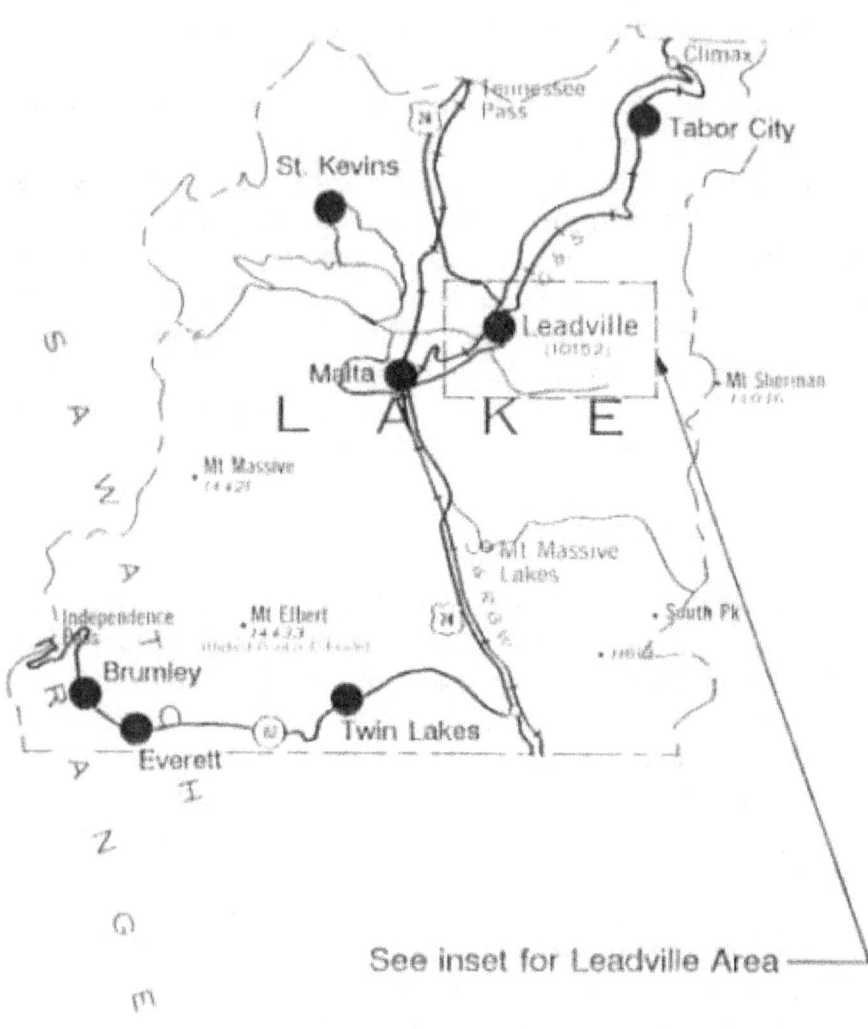

LAKE COUNTY MAP

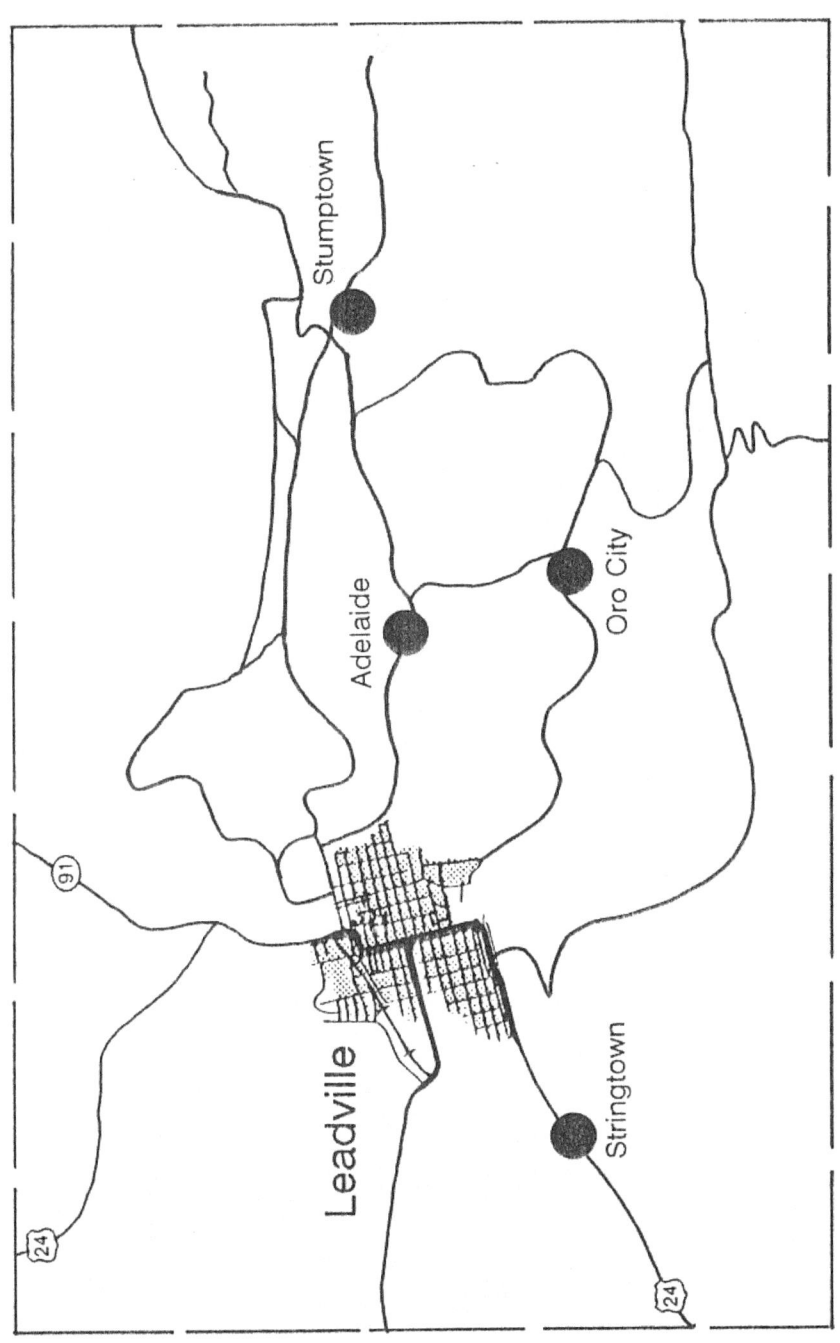

LEADVILLE MAP

Gold, Silver, and the Growth of a City

While prospecting in California Gulch (near the site of present-day Leadville, Colorado) in April of 1860, Abe Lee discovered gold and proclaimed, "Boys, I've got all California here in this pan." The stampede was on. In an effort to grab all of the property which might be potentially profitable, Abe and his group of 14 miners staked nearly the entire gulch with "speculative claims." The plan didn't work. New prospectors demanded a miners' meeting, from which came the official "Bylaws of California Mining District, California Gulch, Arkansas River." They were adopted on May 12, 1860, and established provisions as to the number, size and type of claims which could be filed. Fair laws invited more newcomers. By mid-summer there were 5,000 people with tents and wagons scattered from one end of the gulch to the other. Merchants sold supplies from their wagons. Canvas saloons popped up everywhere. Prostitutes had long lines outside their tents. Finally, some order began to appear. Tents began to "colonize." The original site of Oro City was located on what would become the southern edge of present

California Gulch was the site of the original discovery of gold in the Leadville area. *Denver Public Library, Western History Department.*

day Leadville.

California Gulch yielded over $5,000,000 in gold during the next five years. By 1866, however, the placer gold had dwindled. The heavy black sand was hard to work, and most of the prospectors became discouraged and moved on.

Charles J. Mullen and Cooper Smith, who were grubstaked by a Philadelphian named J. Marshall Paul, found a new rich lode at the Printer Boy Mine, creating a new flurry of activity. The Printer Boy was the first underground gold mine in the Leadville area and marked the transition from surface mining to underground hard rock mining. The remaining inhabitants of the original Oro City dismantled their cabins and moved them, along with their furnishings, to the new location of Oro City, further up the gulch. During the early '70s, however, productivity declined again.

William H. Stevens, who had visited California Gulch in the '60s, was a skilled miner. Alvinus B. Wood was adept in mining engineering and technique. Both men were certain that more progressive mining methods would uncover plenty of gold in California Gulch. Stevens and Wood organized the Oro Mining Ditch and Fluming Company which purchased many mining sites and established many new claims. The partners constructed an 11 mile ditch in order to tap the head waters of the Arkansas River. The new water source was designed to "wash" the sand and gravel in California Gulch. Although it worked, the heavy black sand continued to hamper operations. In 1875, the duo

William H. Stevens was a skilled miner. *Denver Public Library, Western History Department.*

Leadville sprang to life so quickly there were still log cabins in the streets. Pop Wyman's popular saloon is at right.
Denver Public Library, Western History Department.

There were many false-fronted buildings in early Leadville.
Colorado Historical Society.

decided to have the sand assayed. They discovered that it contained 15 ounces of silver per ton and was rich in carbonate. Stevens and Wood kept their find a secret for nearly two years. When the word spread in late 1877, the silver boom was on.

Stevens and Wood had already staked massive claims. The Rock, the Lime, the Stone, the Iron, and the Bull's Eye were holdings in the name of Wood or the Oro Mining Ditch and Fluming Company. Their properties gave them control of Iron Hill and Rock Hill. Stevens and Wood did not discover silver, but their engineering expertise and financial resources were catalysts for the silver boom in Leadville.

The sampling works of August R. Meyer, was one of the primary catalysts in the birth of Leadville. Meyer was backed by Edwin Harrison and his St. Louis Smelting and Refining Company, in Missouri. Meyer convinced Harrison that there was a huge demand for an adequate smelter. Harrison traveled to Leadville and set up shop on the street that was later named in his honor, Harrison Avenue. Shortly thereafter, the St. Louis Smelting and Refining Company began construction of a smelter.

Leadville was a simple community of log structures in 1878. By June of the following year, however, it had blossomed

The Tabor Grand Hotel was called the Vendome for many years.
Colorado Historical Society.

New telephone poles reach for the sky along Chestnut Street in late 1879. *Denver Public Library, Western History Department.*

A wagon full of campaigners stopped to pose for a photographer in front of several gingerbread-laced Victorian homes. *Denver Public Library, Western History Department.*

By 1890, much of the construction along Harrison Avenue was brick and stone. *Denver Public Library, Western History Department.*

In contrast to Harrison Avenue most of Leadville was, and still is, wood frame construction. *Denver Public Library, Western History Department.*

considerably. According to Cass Carpenter, as of May 1, 1879, Leadville had "...19 hotels, 41 lodging houses, 82 drinking saloons, 38 restaurants, 13 wholesale liquor houses, 10 lumber yards, 7 smelting and reduction works, 2 sampling works for testing ores, 12 blacksmith shops, 6 livery stables, 6 jewelry stores, 3 undertakers and 21 gambling houses where all sorts of games are played as openly as the Sunday School sermon is conducted." Additionally, there were 36 brothels. When George E. King and other architects arrived, Leadville took on an air of elegance and sophistication. It wasn't long before Harrison Avenue in downtown Leadville was constructed of predominantly brick and stone.

One of George E. King's projects was the Tabor Grand Hotel distinguished by its French Mansard roof line with arched windows on the upper level. When money became tight during the hotel's construction in 1884, Horace Tabor stepped in with a donation that allowed the structure to be completed the following year. The hotel has operated under several different names, including the Maxwell and the Vendome.

Across the street from the Tabor Grand Hotel another of George King's hotels was constructed. The Delaware Hotel, also with a French Mansard design, was completed in October of 1886 on the northeast corner of Harrison Avenue and 7th Street.

St. George's Episcopal Church on W. 4th Street was built in 1880. Architect Eugene Robitaille designed the structure with Gothic influence. The church bell was donated by Horace Tabor. The Presbyterian Church (now known as "Old Church") was dedicated in December of 1889. The building, located a block north of the Tabor Grand Hotel, was also designed by Robitaille. Many, many fine buildings were erected during the 19th Century and most of them still stand today.

In order to stay abreast of the news, residents of Leadville had several newspapers from which to choose. The *Lake County Revielle* of Richard S. Allen was the first newspaper. It lasted less than two years. The *Herald Democrat*, which sprang from the merger of the *Leadville Democrat* and the *Leadville Daily Herald* in 1886, was a popular choice, as was the *Carbonate Chronicle*. There were many competitors like the *Leadville Dispatch* and the short-lived *Leadville Star*.

Augusta and Horace Tabor

Horace Austin Warner Tabor and Louisa Augusta Pierce Tabor were natives of New England. He was born in Vermont on November 26, 1830, and she in Maine on March 29, 1833. He was a stonecutter, and she the daughter of a contractor. Horace went to work for Augusta's father in Maine. After a lengthy courtship and engagement, the couple was married on January 31, 1857. When he heard news of the earliest gold strikes in the western end of Kansas Territory (an area that would later become Colorado), Horace packed up his family and headed west.

Horace believed that his experience as a stonecutter would give him an advantage in mining. At first, however, he wasn't any luckier than the multitude of other prospectors who had stampeded to the mountains with a dream of riches. When news reached them of Abe Lee's discovery, they headed to California Gulch.

Horace and Augusta were among the earliest arrivals into

Horace Austin Warner Tabor.
Colorado Pioneer Collection.

Louisa Augusta Pierce Tabor.
Colorado Pioneer Collection.

the gulch during the spring of 1860. They were accompanied by their infant son Nathaniel Maxcy. According to Augusta, they arrived on the 8th of May, approximately two weeks after Lee's strike. A food shortage already existed in the gulch. Prospectors had been scrambling to stake claims and failed to take the time to replenish their food supply. Horace Tabor sacrificed his oxen so that hungry miners could eat. By doing so, he immediately became the friend of many. When Augusta indicated she would like to set up a store, the men stopped work and constructed a cabin for her business and the Tabors' lodging. From her cabin, Augusta sold her baked goods and provided meals. She also took in boarders and did laundry. Like most of the men, Horace prospected the surrounding hills. He only did so, however, for a short time. The Tabors owned the only gold scales in the upper end of the gulch. Prospectors brought their dust to the Tabor store to have it weighed.

When placer gold began to dwindle, and prospectors began an exodus from California Gulch, Horace Tabor followed suit. He crossed Mosquito Pass during the fall of 1862 and constructed a cabin in the settlement at Buckskin Joe, two miles west of Alma.

"Buckskin Joe" was the nickname for Joseph Higgenbottom, part-time prospector and part-time trapper. Higgenbottom, who always wore leather clothes, made a placer strike at this location in 1860. A year later he traded his interest in the camp for a horse, a gun, and satisfaction of his bar bill. The community which was named for Higgenbottom, was temporarily renamed Laurette throughout part of the '60s. Buckskin Joe had its own newspaper, stage office, a theater (Laurette Hall), and the Bank of Stansell, Bond and Harris. The popular Pacific House was one of four hotels.

Once his cabin was finished, Horace returned to Oro City and moved his family to Buckskin Joe. Augusta continued her baking and successfully operated a grocery store that also housed the post office. Horace was named postmaster.

The *Rocky Mountain News* once described Buckskin Joe as South Park's "liveliest little burg." Half the residents are said to have made their living from the several saloons, gambling halls, and billiard parlors. From the rowdy mining camp sprang the legend of Silverheels. There may be some truth in this story, then again, it could just be part of Colorado mythology.

During the cold winter of 1861 (before the Tabors arrived), an epidemic of smallpox swept through the mining community. Mines, stores, and saloons shut down. Most of the miners became desperately ill, and many died. There was a steady trek to the little cemetery on the hill, in order to bury the dead. Silverheels, a popular dance hall girl, held her boyfriend as he died in her arms. Requests for nurses went unheeded, for women were not willing to risk their lives or their looks by subjecting themselves to the highly contagious disease which left its victims pockmarked for life. Throughout the ordeal, Silverheels went from cabin to cabin caring for the sick and comforting the dying. She scrubbed, and cooked, and nursed. According to legend, she too was finally stricken by the illness. When the epidemic subsided, miners collected $5,000 in cash as a gift for Silverheels to show their gratitude for what she had done. The men carried the reward to her cabin only to find that she had disappeared. Some time later a woman dressed in black, and heavily veiled, was seen

Wolfe Londoner was one of Leadville's first substantial merchants. The billboard on the side wall of his grocery and hardware may have been Leadville's first. *Denver Public Library, Western History Department.*

in the cemetery – weeping. When approached she fled. Miners believed that Silverheels had come back to mourn her boyfriend and others. For her valor, a majestic peak, Mt. Silverheels, was named in her honor. There was no newspaper in South Park in 1861, nor has anything else been recorded to substantiate the story. The legend, however, has become a part of Buckskin Joe history.

One day while tending the store, Augusta was approached by a man named William Van Brooklyn, who offered to swap his claim for room and board while he started a new business with his mules. Augusta refused the offer. Van Brooklyn subsequently sold his claim for $100 to two prospectors whose yield from the claim approximated $80,000. Disgruntled by the incident, Horace Tabor vowed to grubstake any and all prospectors who requested same, for an interest in their claim.

The success of the Printer Boy, in 1868, enticed the Tabors to return to California Gulch. They brought their store with them. On November 30th of that year, Horace was appointed postmaster of Oro City.

Charles Mater was Leadville's first shopkeeper. In June of

Fryer Hill was the location of several productive mining properties. *Archives, University of Colorado at Boulder.*

1877 he established a mercantile house in a twenty-by-thirty foot log building to the north of the original town of Oro City. By this time, the Tabor's had two stores. One in California Gulch at the second Oro City, and another to the south in neighboring Malta. Realizing the potential of the new area, the Tabors quickly opened a third store, a short distance from Mater's. George Albert Harris, who claimed to be Leadville's first arrival, built the settlement's first hotel. The establishment was known as the City Hotel and would house as many as ten men. Billy Nye, who built the first saloon in Malta, also established the first saloon and billiard parlor in Leadville. A drug store, wagon shop, and sampling works soon followed, and Leadville was on its way.

After naming the settlement Leadville, the camp's forefathers petitioned the postal department to establish a new post office. The Leadville post office became official on July 16, 1877, with George L. Henderson as its first postmaster. Governor John L. Routt issued a proclamation to hold a special election on Tuesday, February 12, 1878. Horace Tabor was elected mayor. During Leadville's first regular election, less than two months later (April 3, 1878) Tabor was re-elected mayor.

George H. Fryer and his partner John Borden were digging

August Rische. *Denver Public Library, Western History Department.*

in an area no one thought would be productive. Working alone one day, Fryer struck good ore. He and Borden called the mine the New Discovery. The location was in an area to be known as Fryer Hill. Soon after the discovery, Borden sold his share to a group of investors. Shortly thereafter, Jerome B. Chaffee purchased Fryer's share for an amount reported to be $50,000. Fryer Hill was also about to make Horace Tabor a very, very wealthy man.

On April 15, 1878, August Rische and George Hook, two German shoemakers, visited Tabor's Leadville store and asked the mayor for a grubstake. Tabor grubstaked Rische and Hook to $17 worth of supplies for a third interest in their findings. He added another $47 worth of tools to the grubstake. The prospectors began digging a few hundred feet north of Fryer's New Discovery. Their intent was to tap the same ore body as Fryer's mine. At a depth of only 27 feet, the pair struck rich ore that would assay at 200 ounces of silver per ton. The Little Pittsburg (spelled without the "h") Mine would make Tabor a millionaire.

Anxious for instant money, Hook sold his share to Tabor and Rische for $90,000. One month later David H. Moffat and Tabor bought Rische's interest for $265,500. After much share trading

George Hook. *Denver Public Library, Western History Department.*

The Little Pittsburg Mine made H.A.W. Tabor a very wealthy man.
Colorado Mountain History Collection.

and financial negotiations, the Little Pittsburg Consolidated Mining Company was organized in November of 1878. The group of Fryer Hill mining properties owned by the new company included the Little Pittsburg and New Discovery. Jerome B. Chaffee was president, David H. Moffat vice president, and H.A.W. Tabor became a member of the Board of Trustees.

"Chicken Bill" Lovell owned an interest in the Chrysolite adjacent to Fryer Hill. After reaching a depth of 20 feet with no success, he decided to try another tactic. Some say he stole a sampling of carbonate ore from the Little Pittsburg and dropped it down his own shaft. The county clerk's records indicate that Horace Tabor paid $10,000 for interests in both the Chrysolite and Carboniferous, on July 13, 1878. Many people snickered when they realized Chicken Bill had pulled a fast one on the Silver King himself, H.A.W. Tabor. Tabor had the last laugh, however. Instead of considering it a bad deal, he further developed the Chrysolite and struck rich silver ore which reaped a bonanza of $3,000,000.

Originally, the first "banking" was done from the Tabor's store. But that would soon change. The Lake County Bank, and the Miners Exchange opened within a few days of each other during April of 1878. Six months later Horace Tabor and August Rische started the Bank of Leadville. It was temporarily housed

The Matchless Mine was possibly the only property Horace Tabor owned without partners. *Colorado Mountain History Collection.*

in a drugstore while the owners constructed a new building. The new Bank of Leadville was one of the finest buildings in the city, and business was brisk. Over the counter business totaled between $75,000 and $90,000 daily.

Western Union brought telephone service to Leadville on May 15, 1879. It connected two of the Malta Smelter Company's plants. Horace Tabor and some other leading businessmen seized the opportunity and organized the Colorado Edison Telephone Company on July 16, 1879. Within six months 250 locations had been connected, with 200 more pending.

During his successful days, Horace Tabor seemed to have an uncanny sense of when to buy, and when to sell. Throughout most of 1878 and 1879, the Little Pittsburg yielded $8,000 to $10,000 per day. In September of 1879 Horace sold his interest to his partners David Moffat and Jerome Chaffee for an even $1,000,000. Soon thereafter, the Little Pittsburg's yield decreased dramatically.

Also in September of 1879, Horace Tabor purchased the Matchless Mine for $117,000, which was possibly the only investment he ever made without partners. After purchasing the property from Tim Foley, A.P. Moore, and T.B. Wilgas, he spent another $30,000 to settle law suits against the property. The following year, the Matchless turned into a bonanza. During the peak years of its operation, the Matchless Mine lived up to it's name, yielding $1,000,000 per year.

    Augusta Tabor was accustomed to a modest life style and did not agree with the lavish tastes that accompanied Horace's new found fortune. He spent or gave away his money almost as fast as he received it. Horace and Augusta grew further apart. It wasn't long before the beautiful divorcee, Elizabeth McCourt Doe caught Horace's eye.

Baby Doe and the Tabor Triangle

Attractive and vivacious Elizabeth Nellis McCourt was born in Oshkosh, Wisconsin on September 26, 1854. Lizzie loved to ice skate and also had visions of one day becoming a great actress. On June 27, 1877, in Oshkosh, she married shy, but dignified William Harvey Doe, Jr.. Immediately thereafter the couple departed for Central City, Colorado, where Harvey's father, Colonel W.H. Doe, Sr. had mining interests. Harvey was to work Colonel Doe's share of the Fourth of July Mine for its profits, with the stipulation that if he was successful the share would be deeded to the newlyweds in a year. Lizzie dreamed of riches. Luck wasn't on their side, however, for the mine failed to produce high-grade ore and their capital was running very low. The couple moved to a small, second-story, two-room apartment in Black Hawk (one mile from Central City) in order to save money. Their debts increased and Harvey became irresponsible. With financial pressures mounting, dissension set in. The dissension

Elizabeth McCourt Doe (Baby Doe Tabor). *Colorado Pioneer Collection.*

The Clarendon Hotel was constructed by H.A.W. Tabor. *Denver Public Library, Western History Department.*

soon turned to quarreling.

Disillusioned, and seeking excitement, Lizzie began hanging out at Central City's flashy variety hall, the Shoo-Fly. To the miners and sporting girls Lizzie became known as Baby Doe. Naturally, she heard all the talk around the Shoo-Fly, and elsewhere, about the meteoric rise of silver and the new fortune of Horace Tabor.

Harvey deserted Baby Doe while she was pregnant. She later gave birth to a stillborn baby. A friend, Jake Sands (whose real name was Sandelowsky) sent the discouraged Baby Doe to Leadville for a "change of scenery." During her visit she heard more and more about Leadville's leading citizen, H.A.W. Tabor. Baby Doe returned to Black Hawk and divorced Harvey on March 19, 1880. Sands, who was a partner in a clothing business, Sands & Pelton, had recently opened a new store on Harrison Avenue in Leadville. Sands moved to the Cloud City in order to run the new business. It didn't take much encouragement for him to convince Baby Doe to follow him. Although they lived in separate boardinghouses, Jake and Baby Doe had a relationship. Her heart wasn't in it, however, and she dreamed of the day she might meet Horace Tabor. Finally she did.

Instantly, there was magic when the two met at the Saddle

Rock Café. Before the evening was over Tabor had written a check to the amazed Baby Doe for $5,000, in order that she might pay off a debt to Jake Sands. Within days Tabor had moved Baby Doe into a suite at the Clarendon Hotel, and they became lovers.

Horace Tabor's leap to wealth and prominence made him potentially attractive for political office. He became the Republican Party nominee for lieutenant governor, and was elected to that post in November of 1878.

When Horace Tabor became lieutenant governor of Colorado, he and Augusta moved to Denver. He paid $40,000 for their home at 17th and Broadway. He also purchased a fine carriage for $2,000. It was said to be an exact replica of one used

Baby Doe Tabor. Seldom has anyone experienced such a contrast of wealth and poverty. *Colorado Pioneer Collection.*

Baby Doe Tabor's two daughters. Elizabeth Bonduel Lillie, age 4 (at left) and Rose Mary Echo Silver Dollar. *Colorado Mountain History Collection.*

at the White House in Washington, D.C.

As lieutenant governor, Horace and Augusta entertained society in their fine new mansion in Denver. His visits to Leadville were frequent, however, and he spent much time with Baby Doe. People talked. Later, Horace moved Baby Doe into a plush suite at the elegant Windsor Hotel in Denver.

Augusta was a plain and simple woman who became increasingly critical of Horace's extravagant way of life as well as his politics. Horace asked her for a divorce, but she refused. When Augusta was absent at the festive opening of the Tabor Grand Opera House, in Denver (September 5, 1881), there were more whispers.

Eventually, in a surprise move, Augusta filed a suit for property settlement, asking Horace for $50,000 per year and their Denver home. Horace had the suit suppressed for being without the jurisdiction of the court. Meanwhile, he obtained a "secret" divorce in Durango, where he was a property owner and had a friend who was a judge. After doing so, there was a question in Horace's mind as to the validity of what he had done. In the developments which followed, Augusta sued for divorce and received a settlement (January 2, 1883) of mining stock, their Denver house, and other real estate.

With Horace gone, Augusta found other outlets to occupy her time. She was very involved in the Unitarian Church. She stayed busy in social circles, and was a founder and officer of the Pioneer Ladies' Aid Society.

When Henry Teller vacated his senatorial post to accept a cabinet position in President Chester Arthur's administration, Horace Tabor was appointed to a 30 day interim term as United States Senator.

These events paved the way for the lavish wedding of Horace and Baby Doe. They were married March 1, 1883, in Washington, D.C. with many dignitaries in attendance, including President Chester Arthur. The ceremony was held at the Willard Hotel.

Unlike Augusta, Baby Doe was extravagant and helped Horace spend his money. The couple lived in grand style for ten years during which time Horace and Baby Doe gave birth to three children. Elizabeth Bonduel Lillie was born July 13, 1884. On October 17, 1888, Baby Doe gave birth to a son who lived only a few hours. Another daughter, Rose Mary Echo Silver Dollar was born December 17, 1889. Baby Doe bought thousand-dollar dresses for her daughters. The fairy tale life, however, would eventually end.

As the '80s drew to a close, lower silver prices threatened to slow production. In an effort to strengthen the failing silver market, the federal government passed the Sherman Silver Purchase Act (July 14, 1890) which authorized the government to issue $54,000,000 in paper money annually, backed by a monthly purchase of 4.5 million ounces of silver. Silver prices, however, continued to slip. Newly elected President Grover Cleveland, an advocate of the gold standard, called a special session of congress on August 1, 1893, during which the Sherman Silver Purchase Act was repealed. The price of silver plunged. The silver crash of 1893 depleted the fortunes of H.A.W. Tabor and others. Horace had refused to take notice of economic indicators that silver was in trouble. Subsequently, he failed to take precautionary measures which might have prevented a total collapse of his empire. His fortune was virtually lost overnight. The Tabors owned real estate but it was heavily mortgaged. The Tabor Opera House, the Clarendon Hotel, the Tabor Block and his interests in several mining properties were seized by creditors. Tabor was temporarily able to hold on to the Matchless Mine and his Eclipse Mine in Boulder County.

Horace Tabor borrowed $15,000 from Winfield Scott Stratton of Colorado Springs, who had extracted millions of dollars in gold from his mines near Cripple Creek. It was a debt that would never be repaid, but eventually forgiven by Stratton. Horace was unemployed for several months. He and Baby Doe received some help from Horace's son Maxcy. They rented a cottage for $30 per month, and learned to live frugally. Winfield Scott Stratton eventually helped Horace land a job as postmaster of Denver. The position paid $3,500 per year. Tabor held the post for 15 months. The man who had been mayor of Leadville, lieutenant governor of Colorado, and briefly a U.S. senator, died on April 10, 1899. He was 68 years old. The cause was

Horace Tabor's fortune was depleted by the silver crash of 1893. *Colorado Pioneer Collection.*

Nathaniel Maxcy Tabor, son of Augusta and Horace. *Colorado Mountain History Collection.*

appendicitis.

In 1892 Augusta Tabor sold her house at 17th and Broadway. She moved across the street to the Brown Palace Hotel. Maxcy and the Tabors' long time friend Bill Bush were the hotel managers and resided there, as well. Augusta eventually headed to California to seek a warmer climate for her failing health. She died in Pasadena, on February 1, 1895, at the age of 62. Her body was returned to Denver where she was interred at Riverside Cemetery. Maxcy inherited his mother's wealth, said to be a million and a half dollars.

Augusta had always believed that one day Horace would come back to her, but it was not to be, for he and Baby Doe remained totally loyal to each other until his death. Later, after returning to Leadville, Baby Doe was abandoned by her daughter Elizabeth. Peter McCourt, Baby Doe's brother, had provided train fare allowing Elizabeth to travel to Oshkosh, Wisconsin. When Elizabeth left, she left for good.

Silver Dollar, Baby Doe's second daughter, had her

In poverty, Baby Doe Tabor spent her remaining years living in a small shack at the Matchless Mine. *Colorado Pioneer Collection.*

mother's good looks and talent for attracting male attention. She was "loose" with the men, and became more and more unmanageable. Believing that Silver Dollar needed a change of scenery, Baby Doe sent her to Denver, where she obtained a job as a reporter for the *Denver Times*. Silver Dollar eventually wrote a novel *Star of Blood*, and a few songs, which netted her very little money. The last time Baby Doe saw Silver Dollar was probably during the month of November in 1914. Silver Dollar died in 1925, at age 36. She was an alcoholic, reliant on drugs, and sold her body for pleasure prior to her death.

In 1906, Baby Doe Tabor moved to a small shack adjacent to the Matchless Mine where she spent her remaining years. One day in 1935, her frozen body was discovered covered in rags and newspapers, in an obvious attempt to stay warm. Seldom has anyone experienced such contrasts of beauty and decay, or wealth and poverty.

Most discussions of Horace and Baby Doe Tabor and the Matchless Mine include a quotation which was supposedly uttered by Horace to Baby Doe while on his death bed, "Hold on to the Matchless." In actuality, Horace Tabor did not own the Matchless at the time of his death. The property went through several different owners, and lessees, and was involved in much litigation. Probably because of her faith in the Matchless, and the fact that she was destitute, Baby Doe and her daughters were allowed to live in the shack at the property that was once the source of much of her wealth. Writer and historian, Caroline Bancroft, confessed prior to her death that she had created Horace's quotation, believing that it would make "good press."

They Made Their Mark

Horace Tabor built both the Clarendon Hotel and the elegant Tabor Opera House in 1879. Many important people and famous stars graced the stage of the Tabor Opera House. Lectures were held by British critic and poet, Oscar Wilde. Wilde raised a few eyebrows by drinking several Leadville miners under the table. Central City's Jack Langrishe and his players performed for the more cultured. The great Harry Houdini performed his magic on stage. Shakespearian actor Laurence Barrett appeared with his supporting cast. Boxing matches were held at the Tabor Opera House, headlined by such prize fighters as John L. Sullivan and James Corbett. John Philip Sousa's Marine Band and actress Sarah Bernhardt were among many to appear at the facility.

Many other people of fame or fortune, or both, left their mark on Leadville – and vice versa. Meyer Guggenheim reaped a bonanza from the A.Y. Mine. He invested into the smelting

The Tabor Opera House. The bridge at right extends to the Clarendon Hotel. *Colorado Historical Society.*

The elaborate interior of the Tabor Opera House. *Colorado Pioneer Collection.*

industry and other properties in which his seven sons all became millionaires as well. David May opened the Great Western Auction House and Clothing Store in Leadville on January 1, 1878. This was the forerunner of the department store chain known as the May Company.

    The successful hardware store of Charles Boettcher was the foundation for another fortune. Boettcher moved his holdings from Leadville to Denver and amassed extraordinary wealth. James Viola Dexter was another man made rich by Leadville's silver. A log cabin which Dexter fixed up as an exclusive private poker club now sits on the property of the Healy House Museum. Dexter was a collector of curios and rare coins. His coins alone were worth over $100,000, a tidy sum in the 1800s. Samuel Newhouse eventually became a copper magnate after he struck it rich in Leadville. The Iron Mask Mine, a lucrative silver producer, at nearby Gilman was developed by Leadville newspaper man Joseph Burnell. The Morning Star Mine added to the riches of two-time governor John L. Routt. The wealthy John F. Campion later developed the beet sugar industry in Colorado. Leadville launched successful financial careers for Marshall Field, W.B. Daniels and many others.

    Plainsman and U.S. government scout, John B. "Texas Jack" Omohundro was born in Virginia in 1846. Following the

Civil War, at age 16, Jack headed west to become a cowboy. He spent much time with the Pawnee Indians and could speak their language. Omohundro was a close friend of Col. William F. "Buffalo Bill" Cody, and was instrumental in helping him start the first wild west shows in America. Jack and his wife, Mlle. Guiseppina Morlacchi resided in Leadville, where on June 28, 1880, he died at the age of 33. Later, when Cody came to Leadville with his Buffalo Bill's Wild West Show, he paid tribute to the memory of his old friend.

During a tour of mining camps in 1877, Susan B. Anthony stopped in town to lecture for women's suffrage. While visiting 24 camps, Anthony was only able to collect $165, a reflection of the unpopularity of the issue. Several men of the cloth left their mark as well, including Father John Dyer (who was the first mail carrier over the Mosquito Range), Father Joseph P. Machebeuf (who made regular visits to California Gulch in the early days), Pastor Arthur Lake, Father Henry Robinson, and the Reverend Tom A. Uzzell. Prostitute and storyteller, Laura Evans, spent about three eventful years in Leadville. Madame Vestal, who operated a dance hall on State Street, was "queen" of the lady gamblers. George Fryer discovered silver on the hill which bears his name, sold his claim, then spent his money as fast as he was able. When his money ran out, he committed suicide. The Maid of Erin

David May. *Colorado Pioneer Collection.*

Price Wanklin, whose shop was on E. 3rd St., was a popular horse shoer during the 1890s. *Colorado Mountain History Collection.*

Mine made Jack McCombe a wealthy man. He spent much of his wealth, however, sending presents to everyone he knew in his home country of Ireland. One of those who made a name for himself because he didn't strike it rich was James Fenton. After working twelve unsuccessful claims, the dejected miner buried himself with a dynamite blast. In 1878, Dr. David H. Dougan closed his office in Alma, crossed Mosquito Pass and set up shop in Leadville. Nobody seemed to need a doctor, however, and Dougan sat in his office for 28 days without a customer. On the 29th day he received word that there had been a mine accident and he was needed immediately. That was the beginning of his illustrious career in Leadville. Dougan was a successful physician, then became mayor in 1881, and later was president of the Carbonate National Bank.

    Louise H. Updegraff was Leadville's first public school teacher. Louise, who's husband was a lawyer, was paid $40 per month (while school was in session) for her instruction. She taught 30 students (there weren't many children in early Leadville) in a small log structure. The original session, that opened in February of 1878, lasted only three months before the school closed due to a lack of funds. The closing was short-lived, however, and it wasn't long before Louise Updegraff's pay had doubled.

Leadville Color

Not only did gold and silver provide color in Leadville, but so did many of its people. The Cloud City certainly had its share of interesting characters.

Irishman, John D. Morrisey, became a favorite topic of conversation around Leadville during the silver boom. His fame wasn't due to his mining success, nor as the result of an all night battle over claim rights at the O'Donovan Rossa property (February 21, 1880), during which thousands of shots were fired but nobody killed. His fame was attributed to his illiteracy. Morrisey couldn't read or write, and his knowledge of mathematics was terrible.

According to one story, Morrisey carried a bottle of whiskey to the portal of one of his mines. He hollered into the shaft, "How many of you are down there?" The reply that came from the shaft was, "Three!" Morrisey yelled back, "Well, half of you come up and have a drink."

On one occasion, Morrisey was approached by one of Leadville's churches and asked if he would donate the money for a new church chandelier. He said that he would, but expressed a concern as to its use, saying, "I'll be damned if I know who would play on the thing."

John Morrisey couldn't sign his name. Being a business man, his signature was often required on papers or documents. He had a number of excuses to avoid signing his name, such as, "My fist is frozen and I can't hold a pen." He once showed up at a hotel with a handkerchief rapped around his hand, and told the clerk, "Just write my name for me, young fellow. I just slammed the buggy door on my hand and hurt it."

He hated to admit that he couldn't write, and in the same manner he hated to admit that he couldn't tell time. Morrisey carried a fancy gold watch studded with diamonds. It had been presented to him for being a successful mine boss. He carried it with pride, but couldn't read it. When asked for the correct time, he would pull out his watch and say, "See for yourself, then you'll know I'm not lying to you." If he wanted to know the time himself, he would approach somebody and say, "I've made a bet with myself on the time of day." He would then pull out his watch and hand it over to the person while he continued his discourse. "I bet with myself that it's 7:35. If I'm right, we'll go into a bar and have whatever you would like to drink or smoke." Morrisey would never guess correctly, so his bet was always safe, but he would find out the correct time.

On one occasion while a resort hotel was being constructed at nearby Twin Lakes, the owners agreed to purchase some gondolas for the use of their guests. They asked Morrisey how many he thought they should buy. His response was, "Just get two and let them breed."

There were many honest people in Leadville, though one wouldn't believe it if he read the newspaper often. Frank W. DeWalt was president of the First National Bank of Leadville before it closed in 1884. He wasn't much of a president. Then again, he wasn't much of a gambler. Evidently, DeWalt gambled away $50,000 and financed the bordello of Madame Winnie Purdy with depositors' money. His wrong doing netted him a prison term.

The Leadville Chronicle had a colorful newsman named Orth Harper Stein. Many of the legends and tall tales which emerged from the region were created by Stein. Stein once wrote that the frozen body of a female prospector had been found north of Saint Kevins, near Homestake Peak. The body was carried to the newspaper office and placed on a desk near a pot-bellied stove. Newsmen watched as the woman thawed out, limb by limb. Once completely thawed, she sat up, then walked out of the office – never to be seen or heard from again.

Some say Stein was a "loose cannon," but he was definitely imaginative. He created a sea serpent in Twin Lakes, an abominable snowman, an underground shipwreck with an Egyptian registry, and the discovery of a man's skeleton with chains wrapped about his neck and bowls of food just out of his reach. When Stein left Leadville, he went to Kansas City where he was involved in a fight over a chorus girl, during which he killed a variety theater owner. For his dastardly deed, he was sentenced to be hanged. Somehow his family was able to obtain a second trial for Orth.

Ultimately he was acquitted. His life, however, continued in a downward spiral. It is said that he stole his mother's jewels and money. He was overtaken with consumption, and died in 1901 in New Orleans.

Formerly a stagecoach driver, Broken Nose Scotty received his name after incurring injuries from a runaway stage near Weston Pass. Scotty was a storyteller and a dreamer. Like so many others in the Leadville area, he turned to prospecting, certain that instant wealth would be in his future. During the week he would diligently work his claim on Breece Hill. During the weekends he frequented Leadville's barrooms where he loved to tell stories of his harrowing experiences as a stage driver.

One Saturday night in 1879, Broken Nose Scotty became very drunk and disorderly. It wasn't long before the stiff arm of the law carried him to the jailhouse and locked him up. The jail was crowded, as it usually was, and he immediately found a new audience for his stories.

The following morning Scotty had a visitor who wanted to buy his claim. They agreed upon a price of $30,000. Scotty was released from jail, and the two went straight to a lawyer's office to draw up the papers. The deal was consummated.

Scotty was ecstatic for he had never seen so much money. He wanted everyone to share his happiness. Gleefully, he returned to the jailhouse and "bailed out" all of his "friends." Together they all went to the haberdashery and were outfitted from head to toe with new clothes. The group proceeded on to the Tontine, early Leadville's most fashionable restaurant. Champagne and the finest meals were ordered for everybody. They ate and drank, then drank some more – and all wound up back in jail for disturbing the peace.

It is said that Broken Nose Scotty provided a trust to take care of his aging mother. Scotty spent the rest of his money and eventually died a pauper, with the county ultimately paying his burial fees.

Reverend Thomas A. Uzzell was always addressed by others as "Parson Tom," but to many he was known as the "Fighting Parson." Uzzell was a clergyman east of the Mosquito Range at the town of Fairplay. When much of his congregation moved to Leadville during the early days of the silver boom, he realized he should also go. He arrived in Leadville on February 1, 1878. With no place to sleep, he rolled out his bedroll in an abandoned dry goods box. It didn't take him long, however, to become established. To all, he announced his intention of building a Methodist Episcopal Church. While he raised money, he preached in saloons and gambling houses.

Parson Tom had a "claim" on a lot on which he planned to construct the church. One day some "claim jumpers" were preparing the lot for mining. Parson Uzzell stripped off his coat and waded into the miners. Later he said, "I made up my mind, if the Lord wanted me to recover that lot He would give me strength to lick those fellows – and He did."

Toughs and Tarts

Most of Leadville's many saloons, gambling dens, dance halls, and brothels were located along State Street and in its dingy corridors. There was Tiger Alley, French Row, Coon Row, and Stillborn Alley. It was one of the most wicked and rowdy areas in the entire Old West. There were elegant bordellos and one-girl cribs. Many of the dance halls and saloons had rooms above where more than just a garter was removed. Tough men, painted women, and slick gamblers could be found at "joints" such as the Bucket of Blood, the Pioneer, the aptly named Red Light Hall, the Carbonate Concert Hall, the National, the Odeon, the Bon Ton, the Bella Union, and the Little Casino. Madams such as Mollie Price, Mollie May, and Sallie Purple ran "houses" which catered to a fairly respectable clientele. In contrast the cribs had girls of every size and shape, and every color and origin, and would cater to anyone. Top prostitutes such as the Pioneer's sassy Maude Deuel could make as much as $200 per week. The Texas House, which was located on the corner of State Street and Harrison Avenue, was one of the largest gambling halls in Colorado. Many fortunes were made in Leadville, and a part of many were spent on State Street.

For the most part, justice in early Leadville left much to be desired. Murder and thievery were commonplace. Vigilantes often took the law into their own hands. Sometimes, the "guilty" were hanged and left swinging for days as an "example" to others. The first person ever jailed for insanity was so judged because he spent all his time in prayer. It was dangerous for an individual to walk the streets at night, even if he had a cocked pistol in hand. Armed guards were stationed at the Presbyterian Church construction site to discourage claim jumpers. Becoming a marshal in Leadville sometimes meant signing your own death warrant. Many a man was shot for a gambling debt, a dispute over a claim, in an argument over a woman (and there weren't many women for a while), during a drunken brawl, or for no reason at all.

At first, law and order (what there was of it) was maintained by the saloon owners and their "bouncers." Leadville's first marshal, T.H. Harrison was run out of town after serving only a few days. He received so many threats from the multitude of bad eggs around town, it convinced him that life would be safer somewhere else. Harrison was replaced by George O'Connor. He wore the badge three and one-half weeks before he met his demise. James M. Bloodsworth, a deputy of O'Connor, had been reprimanded for spending too much time in the town's saloons. Bloodsworth did not like being chewed out and decided to get even with the marshal. On April 25, 1878, a Thursday night, the two came face to face at Billy Nye's Saloon. After having much to drink, Bloodsworth became very belligerent. O'Connor stepped toward the deputy in an effort to calm him down. As he did, Bloodsworth unholstered his revolver and fired several shots at O'Connor. The deputy then dashed from the saloon, stole a horse, and raced out of town. O'Connor died within hours. A reward of $600 was posted for the return of Bloodsworth, but it was never collected.

Tough guy, Martin Duggan, was appointed city marshal. Duggan was an Irishman who arrived in America at a young age.

State Street, and its adjacent alleys, was one of the wildest areas in the early West. *Denver Public Library, Western History Department.*

Dancing girls often adorned the stage at the Grand Central Theatre. Denver Public Library, Western History Department.

After spending much of his youth in New York, he headed for the gold fields of Colorado at age 16. Mayor Tabor knew that it would take a tough individual to deal with all the roughs in town. Duggan lacked diplomacy, but was very strong and fearless. His pay was $125 per month.

Like Harrison and O'Connor, Duggan received several threats, which he disregarded. He established himself in the eyes of the community almost immediately. A rowdy group was making trouble at the Tontine Restaurant, on West Chestnut Street. Duggan spotted a wanted man in the group and called him out. When the man didn't budge, Duggan gave him the alternatives, "Go and live. Stay and die." Realizing that the marshal was dead serious, the wanted man went along without any trouble.

Tom Lavery was a miner who handled a gun fairly well. Lavery had staked a claim and proceeded to work it. The problem was that its location was completely surrounded by property owned by H.A.W. Tabor. When Tabor was unsuccessful in getting Lavery to leave the claim, Duggan and his deputies were summoned to force the miner from the property. Lavery was confronted by Duggan but refused to budge, remaining in the mine shaft with only his head exposed. A gunfight erupted during which Lavery shot down two deputies. Tom Lavery was in turn killed in his own shaft.

Charlie Hines and John Elkins had been arguing. The argument turned into a fist fight. Elkins then pulled a knife and stabbed Hines. Elkins turned himself in to one of the officers and was jailed. Martin Duggan was at home one evening when one of his deputies arrived to inform him that a lynch mob was forming. When the outraged mob rounded the corner near the jail, Marshal Duggan was waiting for them. He stood beneath a lamp post with a cocked revolver in each hand. He told the mob that he would kill the first man who tried to pass the lamp post. Realizing that Duggan was serious, and that some of them might get killed, the crowd used good judgment and dispersed. Hines later recovered. Elkins was quietly released from jail one night and never heard from again.

After successfully completing his one-year term as city marshal, Martin Duggan decided to resign. With Duggan out, and P.A. Kelly in as new city marshal, lawlessness once again ran rampant.

The price of town lots had risen drastically. "Lot-jumpers," using various strong-arm methods, would run property owners out of town then take over their land. Robberies and holdups occurred with such regularity that one local newspaper ran a weekly article called the "Holdup Record." After closing up their shops at night, merchants often carried large sums of money home with them. They were prey for thieves and highwaymen. Banks closed early, and most stores offered little protection against break-ins.

In September of 1879, merchants took matters into their own hands. They organized the Merchants' Protective Patrol, a private police force of eight men who were deputized, but paid by the business owners. Their job was specifically to protect the property of the merchants. They would check doors and windows after hours, and also escorted merchants carrying valuables.

Miners often worked their mines until dark. Accordingly, merchants stayed open quite late to accommodate the miners. On one occasion, Carl Bockhaus closed his barber shop about 10:30 p.m. and headed toward home. He was carrying a substantial amount of cash and a revolver. As he walked west on State Street, Bockhaus was approached by two would-be thieves.

They were later identified as Patrick Stewart and a fellow named Clifford. The pair demanded that the barber throw up his hands. Bockhaus raised his revolver and commenced firing. One slug dropped Clifford where he stood. Another wounded Stewart, who took off down the street, but wouldn't go far. Carl Bockhaus became an instant hero to the merchants and honest people of Leadville. Stewart was jailed, but his story didn't end there.

The 1879 edition of the Leadville City Directory had a listing that read, "Frodsham, E. real estate dealer, res. Tenth avenue, bet. Harrison avenue and Pine Street, Capital Hill" [sic]. Edward Frodsham came to Leadville in 1879 after being acquitted for killing a man in a gunfight in Laramie, Wyoming. He was very involved in the lot-jumping that was occurring around Leadville. He seemed to have some legal basis for his lot-jumping endeavors, feeble as they may have been. Most citizens considered Frodsham a crook, and couldn't wait for the day when he would

Leadville in July of 1879. *Denver Public Library, Western History Department.*

be brought to justice.

Meanwhile, concerned citizens formed a vigilance committee. Nobody knows for sure how many there were, though they claimed to be 700 strong. They met in secret. It is generally assumed that some members of the law were involved. Maybe Pat Kelly, or Ed Watson, or both, plus others. On the 17th of November, 1879, Undersheriff Ed Watson arrested Edward

Frodsham, on a charge that today would be considered "disturbing the peace." He was jailed alongside of Patrick Stewart. Evidently Frodsham was denied bail, probably to assure that he was still there when the vigilance committee paid their visit.

At 1:00 a.m. on the morning of the 20th, Ed Watson was "captured" by a number of vigilantes. They marched him down to the county jail at 5th Street and Harrison Avenue. Watson instructed the guard on duty to unlock the jailhouse door, which he did. Frodsham put up a desperate fight, before he was dragged from the building to the lot next door where he was hanged from the framework of the new jail that was under construction. Patrick Stewart also received the same fate.

As daybreak settled in over Leadville, the two bodies dangled for all to see. Pinned to Frodsham's back was a note that read:

> "Notice to all lot thieves, bunko steerers, foot-pads, thieves and chronic bondsmen for the same, and sympathizers for the above class of criminals: This is our commencement, and this shall be your fates. We mean business and let this be your last warning… and a great many others known to this organization. Vigilantes' Committee. We are 700 strong." [sic]

Following the warning was a list of names of undesirables who were encouraged to leave town. The first evening following the lynchings marked the opening of the elegant Tabor Opera House. Jack Langrishe, and his troupe of players, performed for a nervous, half-filled house, just one block from where Frodsham and Stewart were swinging earlier in the day. A detachment of militia was called upon to help keep the peace. Martin Duggan was reappointed as city marshal the following month. The following April, however, he refused to accept another term, opting instead to operate a livery stable business. Edmund Watson was named his successor.

Winnie Purdy operated an elegant brothel on West 5th Street. She decided to purchase a sleigh, and did so from Martin Duggan. As he set out to deliver the sleigh, Duggan was still fuming from an argument he had earlier with Lewis Lamb. When

Duggan encountered Lamb along the route to Winnie Purdy's place, he stopped to exchange more heated words. Incensed, Lamb continued down the street to Madame Purdy's brothel where he confronted Duggan and demanded an apology. When Duggan refused, Lamb drew his revolver. Duggan was too quick. He jumped from the sleigh, and fired one shot that hit Lamb in the mouth. Lamb's revolver was cocked but he never got off a shot. He was dead. A crowd quickly gathered. Mindy Lamb, Lewis' wife rushed to the scene. As she held her slain husband she looked up at Duggan, who was again sitting in the sleigh, and vowed, "Marshal Duggan, I shall wear black and mourn this killing until the very day of your death and then... I will dance upon your grave." Eight years later she did exactly that. Martin Duggan was acquitted on the grounds of self defense for the killing of Lewis Lamb.

On April 9, 1888 Martin Duggan got into an argument with William Gordon one of the dealers at the Texas House. Bailey Youngson, owner of the establishment, came to his dealer's aid. Duggan, who had been drinking heavily, offered to meet them both outside to "shoot it out." Duggan's friends convinced him to forget the matter and head home. Shortly after he left the Texas House (about 4:00 a.m.) a shot rang out. Martin Duggan was found lying in the dirt. He had been shot in the head but was still alive. Shortly after daybreak Duggan indicated that Bailey Youngson had shot him. He later indicated that he did not know who shot him. A few hours later Martin Duggan was pronounced dead. Yes, Mindy Lamb got her wish. She danced on Martin Duggan's grave.

Crime was rampant in Leadville. The last quarter of 1880 showed that an average of 12 persons per day were jailed for one offense or another, and one was charged with murder every 65 hours.

There are many stories to tell about the soiled doves of Leadville. One of the earliest to arrive into the area was Red Stockings. In sharp contrast to most of the early prostitutes, she was pretty, refined, and educated, and as a result was most in demand in Oro City. She would advertise her wares by riding through California Gulch so that miners could see how attractive she was. She made a small fortune during the summer of 1860, then threw a big party for the prospectors before leaving, never to return. The story of Red Stockings is in sharp contrast to most of Leadville's ladies of easy virtue.

The houses of Mollie May and Sallie Purple were adjacent to each other on West 5th Street. They were rivals and competitors. On one occasion, an argument between the two escalated to the point where a gunfight broke out. The madams, their girls and guests sprayed lead at each others' houses until they all ran out of ammunition, at which time things went back to normal.

Mollie May, whose brothel was two doors down from Winnie Purdy's, where Lewis Lamb was killed, was possibly Leadville's most popular prostitute. Her popularity was due in large part to her kindness and generosity. She became a wealthy woman and contributed on a regular basis to hospitals and churches. She was even able to adopt a child. When Mollie died in 1887, her funeral was one of the largest Leadville had ever seen. Even respectable people like Mindy Lamb attended.

Kate Armstead was a black prostitute who supposedly had a mixture of Sioux blood. She lived on that part of West State Street known as "Coon Row." Kate was a tough, hard, self-centered woman. On one occasion when one of her girls was eaten up with disease, and unable to perform as expected, Kate supposedly threw the girl out her front door to let her die in the gutter. On another occasion, during an argument, a drunken customer sliced Kate's body several times with a straight razor. After she recovered Kate decided to sell her place to her neighbor William Jones who operated a small saloon called Coffee Joes. After spending some time in Red Cliff, Kate returned to Leadville and quarreled with Jones whom she claimed defaulted in their agreement. She swore to Jones that she would burn his place down before she left the city. Later that night, after retiring to his room in the back of Coffee Joes, Jones smelled coal oil and heard a crackling noise coming from the alley between Coffee Joes and the old Armstead house. The fire not only destroyed both properties, but many of the shanties on Coon Row. Kate Armstead vanished, never to be heard of again.

Jefferson Randolph Smith followed the carnival into booming Leadville in the early '80s. He was learning the art of "sleight of hand," the old shell game, and other slick tricks designed to milk a man of his hard-earned money. He learned well from the carnival pros, but the con game that intrigued him the most was run by a fellow named Taylor who had set up shop on 3rd Street. Taylor's game was to wrap 10, 20 or 50 dollar bills around cakes of soap which were rewrapped in their blue squares and shuffled into a large pile of identically wrapped cakes. He then offered the crowd their choice for five dollars. A shill would be the first to try. Naturally, he would find a larger bill wrapped around his soap cake, and would holler with glee. Enthralled by the con game and amazed at how much money Taylor could make, Jeff Smith wanted to learn more. So, he went to work for Taylor as a shill.

When Smith had perfected the soap scam he left Leadville for Denver and set up his own operation near Union Station. He grew a beard to disguise his youthfulness, and became very adroit at his game. It was during this time that Smith earned the nickname "Soapy."

Soapy Smith could also handle a deck of cards, and soon added gambling to his repertoire. He trained others to be con artists, then put them to work for a piece of their action. He hired some toughs to handle the objections of those who were rooked, and to also double as body guards. He eventually moved on to the boom town of Creede, where he virtually ran the "underworld."

John Henry "Doc" Holliday arrived in Leadville during July of 1882. Silver mining had already peaked and the economy was beginning to decline. Holliday's health was poor. He had been diagnosed as having consumption (tuberculosis) nine years earlier. He recently had several bouts with pneumonia. By the time he reached Leadville his tubercular coughing fits became more prevalent and he had lost a considerable amount of weight. Holliday loved to gamble, but as his condition worsened, dependence on alcohol increased. The more he drank, the less effective he was at the faro tables.

Johnny Tyler was a ruffian, constantly looking for trouble. Back in Tombstone, Arizona, in October of 1880 (about two weeks prior to the famed gunfight at the O.K. Corral), Tyler and Holliday squared of at the Oriental Saloon. Both men were immediately disarmed by saloon owner Milt Joyce and others. Joyce confiscated their firearms. Doc exited the saloon, then returned a few minutes later brandishing another pistol. Joyce struck Holliday

John Henry "Doc" Holliday, the deadly dentist. *Lowndes County Historical Society and Museum.*

with a gun barrel, then wrestled him to the floor. During the tussle several shots were fired. Milt Joyce received a slug through his left hand while one of his partners, William C. Parker, was shot in the left foot. Tyler hated Holliday, and the feeling was mutual.

Now they were both in Leadville and time had not softened the grudge. One evening in July of 1884, while dealing faro at Hyman's Saloon, Doc was called upon to draw by Johnny Tyler, and several of his cohorts. When Doc advised Tyler and the others that he had no gun, they harassed and insulted him. Tyler had a friend named Billy Allen. Allen was a part-time policeman who was also a friend of Ike Clanton in Tombstone. Clanton was a bitter rival of Holliday. Doc Holliday had borrowed five dollars from Billy Allen. Doc may have borrowed the money with the intention of never paying it back in order to cause trouble. Allen had issued an ultimatum to Doc that the debt must be paid by noon Tuesday, or else. He may have made the loan in an effort to force a confrontation. When Tuesday arrived Doc claimed that he didn't have the money to pay back the loan. He certainly could have borrowed five dollars from a number of people had he really wanted to pay back the loan. Doc heard that Billy Allen was carrying a revolver, and that he would be coming to Hyman's to pay him a visit. To avoid being arrested for carrying a gun (there was an ordinance in effect against carrying firearms), Doc had his revolver hidden beneath the bar. He then took a position from which he could easily reach his weapon. When Billy Allen entered the saloon, his hand was in his pocket. Under the assumption that Allen had a pistol concealed, Doc grasped his revolver and fired twice. The first slug hit Allen in the arm and the second hit nothing. The bartender grabbed Doc and his weapon. Holliday was arrested and jailed. He was released on bail when friends posted his bond. Doc was in and out of court for seven months before the case was resolved by a verdict of "not guilty" (March 21, 1885).

    Holliday's tuberculosis continued to worsen. He believed that hot sulphur springs might help stop the progression of his illness. Doc left Leadville and traveled to Glenwood Springs in May of 1887. He sent for his long-time lady friend, Kate Elder (whose real name was Mary Katherine Haroney). Kate depleted her monetary savings in order to pay expenses when Doc became incapable of working. She remained with him through his final days. John Henry Holliday died on November 8, 1887.

The Suburbs

In 1876 the Adelaide Mine was located in Stray Horse Gulch. The town of Adelaide grew up in the flat valley near the mine of the same name, east of Leadville. Although Adelaide was only two miles from Leadville and the route looked like one continuous town, the "suburb" had its own identity. The town had a post office, school, large smelter, and twenty-eight commercial buildings which included several saloons and stores. By 1879 Adelaide had a population of about 1,000. In addition to the Adelaide Mine, the Eureka, Humboldt and Morning Glory all produced well.

Two of the mines in the vicinity had a problem keeping workers. Senator Gallagher's Mikado and Camp Bird (not to be confused with the one at Ouray) were said to be haunted. A ghost appeared, so they say, and miners quit. Gallagher was killed in the Moyer Mine near Oro City. According to legend, his spirit made the rounds of his mining properties on a regular basis.

When the silver market became rocky, gold producers like the Black Prince Mine helped sustain things. For the most part, the Adelaide area followed the same pattern of deterioration as did most of Leadville's suburbs.

Finntown was situated between Leadville and Adelaide. It's population was predominately Finnish – hence the name.

A short distance above Adelaide was the location of the famous Little Jonny (there is no "h") and the other Ibex mines. The Little Jonny made fortunes for John Campion and J.J. Brown. The Ibex Camp served the several properties of the Ibex Mining Company.

The road up Little Stray Horse Gulch leads to the site where the small community of Evansville once existed, and on to Stumptown. Stumptown (originally named Stumpftown for Joseph Stumpf) is very similar to most of the camps in the area. Wherever there was a cluster of mines, a settlement usually sprang up, and some were very close together. Such was the case with Stumptown. The camp was located in South Evans Gulch a half-mile east of Evansville. Like it's neighbor down the gulch, Stumptown had several saloons and other businesses. The most popular was a pool hall, where the betting was usually heavy.

There were many productive mines in the vicinity. The Boulder, St. Louis, Louise, Winnie, Ollie Reed, Favorite, Little Bob, and the Miner Boy were some of the best. In the 1890s a squabble broke out between the Miner Boy and the Colorado Prince properties. Violence ensued and both mines were burned. Cooler heads finally prevailed and the claims were consolidated and operated by the St. Louis Tunnel.

Stumptown began in 1879 when carbonate ores were discovered in the Little Ellen Mine. The camp boomed until the silver crash of 1893. It experienced a rebound in 1895 but began a gradual decline thereafter. The site was abandoned by the late 1930s.

South of Leadville stretched a group of "suburbs" once known as "Smelter Valley." Jacktown (which had a bowling alley), Stringtown, Bucktown, and Little Chicago (across the river) were blue collar towns. In sharp contrast to some of the Victorian gingerbread in Leadville, Stringtown and its neighbors were comprised of many tenement shacks and plain cabins mixed with a

Adelaide City in Stray Horse Gulch. *Colorado Mountain History Collection.*

Employees pose at the Little Jonny, catalyst for the wealth of J.J. Brown and many others. *Colorado Mountain History Collection.*

few commercial buildings. The many chimneys of the smelting furnaces revealed their main source of prosperity.

The giant Arkansas Valley Plant, a lead smelter, sprawled out between Stringtown and Bucktown. Most of Stringtown's residents were Arkansas Valley workers, as were those of Bucktown and Little Chicago. Founded in 1879 as the Billing and Eilers Smelter, the Arkansas Valley Plant was operated by the American Smelting & Refining Company. Several other smelters operated in the vicinity. Stringtown had a hotel – the Great Northern. There were many saloons, and cribs occupied by the girls of the night – and day.

Additionally, there was the second Oro City, located about three miles southeast of Leadville in California Gulch. The original Oro City (south) and Tintown (just north of the original downtown area) were gobbled up by Leadville.

Rich ore containing silver and lead was accidentally discovered in 1871 by three men trying to find a mountain trail. The men were disappointed because only a trace of gold was found in the ore. Nevertheless, they went to work on their claims, and the Homestake region was born. A small smelter was built in 1875 to process the ores from the region. The site, named Swilltown (four miles southwest of downtown Leadville), was later to be named

Malta. The Swilltown smelter was the first to handle silver in the whole Leadville area.

In 1879, at a cost of $5,000, a race track was constructed at Malta. Its horse races were popular and drew a fine crowd from Leadville and the surrounding area. Alcoholic beverages were important to the economy. There were many saloons and also a brewery. Malta peaked about 1881, but as larger and more efficient smelters appeared closer to Leadville, Malta became less significant.

In addition to Leadville and its suburbs, Lake County had a few other communities worthy of mention. Twenty-one miles southwest of Leadville, in the shadow of Mt. Elbert (Colorado's highest peak) the mining camp of Dayton was established in 1863. Just a short distance from Dayton, the Ryan House was constructed during the same year. It is the oldest stagecoach stop in Colorado. Dayton, which was the county seat for almost two years, eventually phased into the area around the Ryan House to become the resort town of Twin Lakes. Concord stages made the regular run from Leadville to Twin Lakes. Passengers traveling to the boom town of Aspen would transfer to a canvas-top stage for the grueling run over Independence Pass (known then

A majority of Stringtown's residents were employed at the huge Arkansas Valley smelting operation. *Denver Public Library, Western History Department.*

Bullion and workers in "Smelter Valley." *Denver Public Library, Western History Department.*

as Hunter's Pass).

Of several hotels, the Inter-Laken was the most popular. It featured a luxurious dining room, ball room, and gaming hall. The Inter-Laken was expensive with rooms renting for as much as $4 per day.

Leadville mine owner John Campion constructed a magnificent palace facing the lakes. It was lavishly furnished with European finery. Many people were elegantly entertained at Campion's Lodge. During its peak years, tourists always outnumbered the 200 permanent residents of Twin Lakes.

West of Twin Lakes were the settlements of Brumley and Everett. Amidst productive mining on Mount Campion, Star Mountain, and in Mountain Boy Gulch, blossomed the camp of Bromley Station, named for the newly constructed hotel and its owner. The name was shortened to Bromley, and then mysteriously became Brumley. Of the mines in the area, the best producer was the Mount Campion, so dubbed for the mountain on which it was located. A three-mile long aerial tram was constructed at a cost of $115,000 to lift ore over the top of the peak and down to Halfmoon Gulch where it was hauled off by wagon. The town was never very large but it was an important stage stop. The Independence Pass Road was a toll road, and Brumley served as a toll gate.

The Halfway House was an important stagecoach stop on the road over Independence Pass. C.M. Everett platted a town and named it after himself. In addition to several stores and many cabins, there was a two-story stage station and hotel named the Everett House. C.M. Everett built two stamp mills at the confluence of North Fork and South Fork of Lake Creek to crush ores packed in from the Ruby Mine and others. Later, when the railroad arrived in Aspen, the pass became much less useful. As wagon and stage travel declined, so did mining, and so did the settlements of Brumley and Everett.

Realizing he would never become rich working as a carpenter for the Colorado Central Railroad, Thomas Walsh turned to prospecting. His diggings carried him to many areas, and eventually to the spot seven miles northwest of Leadville where he made a good silver strike. In the mid '80s he, and others, platted the town of Saint Kevins (pronounced with a long e) just north of the area which is now Turquoise Lake. There were several productive mines in the area. The Saint Kevins, Griffin, Amity, and President all mined the silver, lead and copper deposits in the area. There

The Inter-Laken Hotel at Twin Lakes. *Denver Public Library, Western History Department.*

John F. Campion made a fortune from the Little Jonny. *Colorado Pioneer Collection.*

was even a little gold. A stamp mill was constructed at the camp. Saint Kevins had a boardinghouse, school, and mercantile store, but the camp never grew very large. Most of the inhabitants left following the silver crash of 1893, as did Thomas Walsh. What Walsh lost due to the devaluation of silver, was a drop in the bucket compared to the fortune he would later realize from the famous Camp Bird Mine near Ouray, that eventually became the second largest producer in Colorado.

Thomas and Carrie Walsh had one daughter, the flamboyant Evalyn Walsh McLain who wrote a book entitled *Father Struck it Rich*. When Evalyn married Edward B. McLain, who's family owned the Washington Post, the newlyweds received $100,000 from each family as a wedding gift. Later, Evalyn purchased the famous Hope Diamond which she dangled in front of Washington and Denver society.

Leadville, and its suburbs, were a unique mixture of many different nationalities and races. The area was not necessarily an ethnic melting pot though, because groups had a tendency to congregate with their fellow man. Nearly fifty percent of the area was other than white American. Most of the African-Americans

Mine dumps and shacks intermixed as shown here on Carbonate Hill. *Denver Public Library, Western History Department.*

congregated on West State Street (2nd Street) in the sector called Coon Row. A majority of the Cornish resided in Jacktown, near the smelters. Most of the Finns, Swedes and Norwegians lived in Finntown or on Chicken Hill. Although they lived in close proximity to each other, the Norwegians and Swedes didn't associate or worship with each other. There was a Lutheran congregation for the Swedes and another for the Norwegians. For the most part, the large Irish contingent congregated on East 6th Street, in Stray Horse Gulch. Many Jews left their mark, especially on Harrison Avenue, as successful merchants. The Americans, Canadians, and English (with the exception of the Cornish) lived in Leadville or near the mining properties where they worked. There was a large contingent of Germans, and many Frenchmen and Italians. There were lesser numbers of Spaniards, Swiss, Danes and Scots. Chinese were totally banned from Leadville during the early years. City fathers did not trust the Chinese and believed that their exclusion would prevent potential labor problems. Soon after they were permitted into the area, three Chinese workers were hanged, then shot repeatedly by vigilantes before being dumped into an empty prospect hole.

A short-lived suburb, Camp Hale, was constructed by the United States Army north of Tennessee Pass during World War II for the purpose of mountain training (the forerunners of the 10th Mountain Division, U.S. Army).

Legends of Lost Gold

Somebody once said, "Prospecting is a game of lost and found. More lost than found!" One of the earliest stories of a lost mine originated a few miles south of Oro City in the early 1860s. A group of prospectors found a rich vein above Cache Creek in an area that later became known as Lost Canyon. Evidently, they worked the mine during the fall of 1860, then again in '61. They returned to the site in the summer of 1862 but could not find the vein. One night years later, in a Granite saloon, a heavily intoxicated prospector claimed that he had found the lost mine, and showed his buddies a handful of rich ore to prove it. The prospector then went on a week-long binge, after which he could not remember how to get back to the mine. The mine in Lost Canyon remains lost, or does it? Someone else could have staked a claim on that vein, and the drunken prospector would never have known, for he didn't know where it was anyway.

Prospector Marc Jones was very superstitious. He believed that when a handful of wooden matches was scattered, if seven match heads ever pointed in one direction, a rich vein could be found along that line. Jones and his partners, Heon Hastings and John Anson, had been mining for some time west of Leadville on Sugar Loaf Mountain. All of their ore was low-grade, but their hopes remained high. They were certain that one day they would strike it rich. Each night when the trio returned to their cabin, Jones would scatter his matches on the table. There were times when as many as six match heads pointed in one direction, but six wasn't enough. Then one day it happened, he tossed the matches and seven lined up perfectly parallel with their heads pointing south toward Mount Elbert. The following morning, Jones packed up to follow his strange compass. He asked his partners to travel with him but Hastings and Anson would have none of his foolishness.

Several days went by before the hungry and bedraggled Jones returned. Hastings and Anson had never seen such a broad grin on his face. Jones pulled a handful of yellow nuggets from his pocket. He also brought back two sacks of dirt which had the best gold content the trio had ever seen. Jones told his partners how he followed the seven matches which led him up a narrow canyon, through a wide gorge, and onto a high-mountain meadow. On a hillside beside the meadow, Jones found the ruins of an old tunnel. Some timbers had fallen and were blocking the entrance to the old mine. Jones was certain that the seven matches had led him to this spot. It took him a full day of clearing before he could enter the mine. Jones further explained that he could pick up the plentiful samples at random and that he believed he had found a bonanza.

Anson and Hastings accompanied Jones to Leadville to have the samples assayed. The tests showed the ore to be rich in gold content. The assayer filled out a card which contained the date June 2, 1882, Marc Jones' name, the test results and the name of the mine – the South Paw Mine. When asked how he arrived at the name Jones explained that his left hand was the best friend he ever had – that it had provided for him all his life – so he named the old mine after his best friend. Shortly thereafter Jones, Hastings and Anson packed up and set out for the South Paw. The trio followed the course that Jones had originally taken as dictated by the seven matches. Once again, Jones reached the narrow canyon, this time with his partners following. Suddenly there was a small rock slide above. Jones was struck on the head and knocked unconscious. When he finally regained consciousness, Marc Jones didn't know his friends. In fact he didn't know anything about the South Paw Mine. The injury had caused amnesia. Marc Jones' memory never returned and he died without being able to tell anyone the location of the South Paw. Heon Hastings and John Anson spent the next six years searching for the mine, but never found it.

Years earlier a man named Robert Jeffrey had located a claim in Lackawanna Gulch, near Mount Elbert. Having heard stories of claim jumpers taking over properties after the original locator disappeared, Jeffrey decided to disguise his mine entrance before he left to visit his family in Missouri. Jeffrey took ill and died leaving only a crude map and vague description as to the location of his claim. A nephew later attempted to locate the mine, but was unsuccessful. Could this have been the tunnel that Marc Jones found using his unusual technique of aligning matches?

Many years later gold ore was found in generally the same area as the lost mine of Lackawanna Gulch and the South Paw. Could this property, called the Mount Champion, have tapped the same vein as those lost mines?

At a location about thirty miles northwest of Leadville (on a crow-fly) occurred what perhaps is Colorado's most authentic tale of buried treasure. In 1849 Buck Rogers and a group of prospectors left Illinois to join the gold rush in California. During their trek through present-day Colorado, the party found traces of gold near a peak they called Slate Mountain. While the others ventured on, six of the prospectors, including Buck Rogers, remained to work the area. Their efforts were rewarded when a rich vein was located. Gold was extracted which they estimated as worth up to $100,000. The ore was stored in a snow drift until such time as it could be packed out.

When provisions ran low, Rogers set out with $500 in nuggets and dust for the nearest camp (which then was 150 miles away). The others remained in what may have been Colorado's first gold camp. After struggling through blizzards for many days, Rogers reached his destination. Winter storms and warm saloons delayed his return trip for several weeks, but finally he departed. Upon returning to the location of the strike, Rogers was horrified at what he saw. An avalanche had carried snow and mud down the mountainside, burying the camp, the men, and the gold. Following the incident, Rogers became a mental wreck, and he tried to drown his conscience in whiskey. He spent his remaining years wandering from one saloon to another telling his woeful tale to anyone who would listen.

Forty years later amid new discoveries in the area, a settlement cropped up which was later to become Fulford. The camp was so named following the tragic death of Arthur H. Fulford – which is another chapter in the Buck Rogers story. While operating a stage stop on the road from Eagle, Fulford had a visitor who claimed to have found human bones, tools, and a treasure of nuggets at a location which sounded much like the description of Slate Mountain. He had covered his discovery and was looking for a partner to help him pack out the gold. Fulford agreed to help. As they prepared for their trip, a strange twist occurred in the story. The visitor was killed in a saloon brawl.

For months, Fulford combed the gulches of the East Fork of Brush Creek, but to no avail. One day, while prospecting on nearby New York Mountain, fate dealt him the same cards that it did Buck Rogers' group years earlier. On New Year's Day 1892, an avalanche swept Fulford to his death.

During the ensuing years, many prospectors combed the area of the east fork of Brush Creek. As far as we know, no one has ever found the location of Buck Rogers' strike. Possibly one day someone will.

The Firefighters

Thousands of miners and hundreds of merchants flocked into the boomtown of Leadville in the late '70s. As they did, canvas structures and log cabins popped up everywhere. Once sawmills were established, wooden structures lined the streets of downtown. The danger of fire existed from the beginning. Leadville wasted no time in establishing volunteer fire brigades. During the spring of 1879 a dangerous forest fire rapidly approached Leadville. Volunteers were called upon to dig trenches and build backfires. As flames approach the north edge of town, the wind direction changed and Leadville was spared. City fathers quickly realized that more precautionary measures were necessary. Before the year's end, Leadville had a new fire tower, alarm system and fire hydrants scattered throughout the city. During the first winter, however, the hydrants were rendered useless, because the pipes froze. By the following summer the pipes had been lowered and wrapped in order to keep water flowing during the cold winters.

Holidays were a time to be festive and the fire department was often very involved on those occasions. The Leadville Fire

A fire department hose cart team on Harrison Avenue.
Colorado Mountain History Collection.

Department's first annual Christmas Ball was held at the Central Station Hall, December 23, 1879, at a lofty price of $5.00 per couple. Fourth of July festivities drew the largest crowds. Fire brigades, or hose companies, would try to out-shine each other during the annual parade, and out-perform each other in the race competition.

On May 19, 1882, a blaze reduced one city block of downtown Leadville to ashes before the hose companies could control the fire. The fancy Hotel Windsor was destroyed along with several buildings. Citizens and merchants alike were irate at the poor performance of the firefighters. They believed that the fire could have been controlled sooner had not several of the firemen been in a state of drunkenness. The city council wasted little time in dissolving the volunteer force, and replacing it with a new salaried fire department. Reliable members of the volunteer brigades were naturally hired immediately. Accusations ceased, as the "new" fire department performed with a higher degree of professionalism.

Firefighters were an important part of every parade, such as this one on Harrison Avenue. *Colorado Mountain History Collection.*

Cloud City Society

Social acceptance in Leadville was based more on wealth than any other factor, but other factors were important. The degree of education and sophistication were not as necessary as they were in an eastern city but nonetheless there were rungs on the social ladder. In addition to wealth, in order to be accepted in Leadville's social circles, a man needed a real "lady" by his side. In addition to proper dress, which included diamonds and jewelry, and elegant gowns and hats, it helped for her to have that Bostonian "air" about her. Her proper handling of gloves, handkerchiefs, fans and parasols would convey the right impression. Body language, whether walking or waltzing, would send a message, as would proper etiquette at an afternoon tea.

Mr. And Mrs. Roswell Eaton Goodell and their five daughters were the perfect model to follow. With regard to the strata of Leadville's society they sat on the top rung of that social ladder. The Goodell sisters, Annie, Mary, Jennie, Clara, and Olive, all had

The Goodell ladies were cultured and sophisticated. *Colorado Mountain History Collection.*

The Mandolin and Guitar Club was one of many musical organizations in Leadville. *Colorado Mountain History Collection.*

impeccable social credentials. They were sophisticated, cultured and though it had no bearing on their social status, attractive. To have received an invitation to an R. E. Goodell gathering was an indication of social acceptance. One such social event was the wedding of Mary Goodell to James Benton Grant at Saint George's Episcopal Church, on January 19, 1881. The groom, who was owner of the Grant Smelter, contributed the funds necessary to complete construction of the church in time for the lavish ceremony.

There was much to do in Leadville for entertainment and recreation. The Tabor Opera House hosted plays, musical productions, boxing matches, lectures, and magic shows. Drama clubs and comedy clubs performed at other locations. Dances were held for every occasion, and when there was no occasion, they made up one just to hold a dance. Every club, it seemed, had their own annual dance, and there were many clubs.

Gentlemen would court their ladies at dances, picnics, and with romantic carriage rides into the adjoining countryside. Twin

Lakes, and the spas at Evergreen Lakes and Soda Springs were popular destinations. There were circuses and carnivals, and for the sport enthusiast a horse track and baseball team. Touring throughout the state, in 1882, the Leadville Blues won 49 of their 52 games. The Leadville Athletic Association had a bowling alley, gymnasium, and boxing ring. Rock drilling contests were popular, as were bicycle races (once the bicycle was invented).

The Leadville Drum Corps, 1897. *Colorado Mountain History Collection.*

The Iron Horse

Robert W. Spotswood and William McClelland brought their Denver and South Park Stage Line from Colorado Springs to Leadville in 1877. They used fine Concord coaches drawn by four-horse teams. In addition to the mail, they could carry a dozen passengers inside and a few more outside, depending upon the amount of luggage and freight. Spotswood and McClelland had two competitors during the short-lived stagecoach era, that only lasted about four years. Barlow and Sanderson ran a more southerly route to Cañon City, while Wall and Witter used the same routes as Spotswood and McClelland. The Denver and South Park Stage Line was the most active, with two coaches running each way daily.

Silas W. Nott built a new road, and established a stage line from Georgetown to Leadville. He also used Concord coaches with six–horse teams. The new line opened in June of 1879, but was short-lived. In 1880 the Denver & Rio Grande Railroad put Leadville's stagecoach operators out of business.

The people of Leadville had demanded a railroad, and railroad owners were anxious to tap the mines and smelters of the Cloud City. The race was on.

Royal Gorge was a natural for a railroad route from Pueblo to the boomtown of Leadville. Both the Denver & Rio Grande and Santa Fe Railroads wanted the route. A fierce confrontation arose between the two. Tempers flared, and suits were filed for the right to lay track through Royal Gorge. Stockholders of the Denver & Rio Grande opted to lease part of their line to the larger Santa Fe Railroad. It wasn't long, however, before the Denver & Rio Grande accused the Santa Fe of violating terms of the lease agreement. The D & RG declared the lease null and void, and demanded the return of their property.

Furious, the Santa Fe brass brought in hired guns including such notables as Ben Thompson and Bat Masterson, who was currently the sheriff of Ford County, Kansas. Armed with

The Denver, South Park and Pacific along side the Denver & Rio Grande at Freemont pass north of Leadville. *Colorado Mountain History Collection.*

a state court order, and supported by local law enforcement, D & RG president General William Palmer had nearly 100 of his workers deputized.

On June 11, 1879, the Santa Fe hired guns barricaded themselves into several railroad buildings at Pueblo. Bat Masterson, and most of the hired guns, manned the roundhouse. With a cannon which had been taken from the armory nearby, it looked much like a fortress. Realizing that the Santa Fe contingent had segmented themselves, the deputies first stormed the telegraph office. One of the hired guns, Harry Jenkins, was shot to death, and the others quickly surrendered.

The deputies then turned their attention to the roundhouse, but they realized it wasn't going to be quite so easy. The cannon was an equalizer. In order to avoid unnecessary bloodshed, the deputies decided to wait them out. Later in the afternoon Bat Masterson and Denver & Rio Grande officials agreed to talk. Following the meeting Masterson and his men surrendered the railroad properties to the D & RG. Being a peace officer himself, Masterson probably accepted the state court order as law. Regardless, the Denver & Rio Grande eventually rode the rails through Royal Gorge.

Meanwhile the Denver, South Park and Pacific was laying its rails up Platte Canyon, following the North Fork of the South

Platte River. The Denver & Rio Grande was first to roll into Leadville. It arrived at 10:00p.m. on July 22, 1880, to a huge celebration. Former President and Mrs. Ulysses Grant stepped off the train to a rousing welcome and a one-hundred gun salute. Grant had just completed two terms in the White House three years earlier and the couple was on a world tour. Although it was late, Grant spoke briefly to the crowd from a platform that had been erected in front of the Clarendon Hotel.

The Denver, South Park and Pacific was right on the heals of the D & RG, but they encountered problems. When they couldn't obtain a suitable right-of-way, they leased (for a term of five years) the right to use the D & RG rails between Buena Vista and Leadville.

Leadville's third railroad, the Colorado Midland, arrived into Leadville on August 31, 1887. Unlike its narrow gauge predecessors, the Midland was a standard gauge, and offered passenger service to and from Colorado Springs.

The Colorado Midland had also encountered right-of-way problems as it neared downtown Leadville. The Denver & Rio Grande refused to sell a piece of property situated in the path of the Midland's approach. Obviously, they intended to impede the latter's progress. Late Saturday, when the clock struck midnight Colorado Midland workers began laying track across the D & RG property. The mayor and members of the police force

The Union Pacific depot on September 29, 1892.
Denver Public Library, Western History Department.

stood nearby to assure that there would be no trouble. It would have been impossible for the D & RG to get an injunction to stop the progress as the courts were closed on Sunday. By Monday morning the track had been laid. Eventually the Midland was able to purchase the property, and the site became the location of their fine Victorian passenger depot.

Railroading peaked about 1894 with some 16 passenger trains serving the Cloud City daily. The old iron horse had changed dramatically since its inception, and subsequently changed the way of life around Leadville.

Labor Disputes

By 1879, mine workers were becoming disgruntled with their wages of $3.00 per day, for a 12 hour day, and poor working conditions. Mine owners were reaping immense profits at the workers' expense. Union talk surfaced. Workers wanted increased pay, better hours and greater mine safety. Mine owners flatly refused the demands.

In 1880 a fire broke out at the Chrysolite Mine that took days to bring under control. Some believed that disgusted workers might have been responsible for the blaze. Horace Tabor drew a hard line with Chrysolite workers. Threats flew back and forth. Mine owners organized private militia companies, and threatened to lower wages to $2.75 per day. Chrysolite miners, led by their spokesman Michael Mooney, went on strike (May 1880). They convinced workers at other mining properties to walk off the job. Sympathetic workers at the smelters followed suit and soon there were nearly 10,000 men on strike. Strikers attempted to picket the Chrysolite but were forcibly repelled by Tabor's private militia, the Tabor Light Cavalry. The situation in Leadville became very tense indeed. Horace Tabor convinced Governor Frederick R. Pitkin to proclaim marshal law and send in the state militia. The militia was commanded by David J. Cook, a former city marshal of Denver, who took matters into his own hands. A 10:00 p.m. curfew was established and all the saloons were closed. A plot by vigilantes to lynch Michael Mooney and other union leaders was foiled.

David Cook kept a tight control on Leadville. When things finally quieted down, he arranged for a meeting between mine owners and union leaders. Mine owners refused to budge, and union leaders finally gave in. Workers returned to their mines at the old wage scale of $3 per day.

During the ensuing years, the Western Federation of Miners became a force to be reckoned with. After accepting low wages and poor working conditions for years, union workers went

An armed guard stands watch at the Robert Emmet Mine, the scene of a battle between mine guards and striking miners on September 21, 1896. *Colorado Mountain History Collection.*

on strike, June 21, 1896. The timing was poor. Mine owners were attempting to rebound from the silver crash that closed many properties just three years earlier. With 2,300 union miners off the job, owners began hiring scabs (replacement workers) in order to keep their mines open. Violence ensued. Union members dynamited the fuel tank at the Coronado Mine. The fire quickly spread to other structures. A fireman from Leadville Hose Company No. 2 was shot to death while fighting the blaze. Once again, the state militia was called upon to quell the anarchy. Most of the mining activity in the district had ceased for nearly three months before Governor Albert W. McIntire's proclamation brought in the soldiers. Work resumed on a very limited basis, predominantly with scabs. The Western Federation of Miners called off their strike on March 9, 1897. Once again, the union had lost, and the strike had lasting repercussions because many of the union workers were never rehired. Water had to be pumped out from many flooded mines before work could resume again.

Although it didn't rival the silver boom, the turn of the century ushered in a new era with over 4,000 miners employed, and the highest gold production in the district's history.

J.J. and the Unsinkable Mrs. Brown

Margaret Tobin was born in Hannibal, Missouri on July 19, 1867. She was the fourth of six children born to Irish immigrant John Tobin. Maggie as she was known in her earlier years, grew up in Hannibal, but couldn't wait to leave. Mary Ann Landrigan, Maggie's half-sister, moved to Leadville in 1883, during the silver boom. Maggie was working as a waitress at Hannibal's Park Hotel when Mary Ann beckoned. It was all the encouragement Maggie needed. She and her elder brother Daniel packed their suitcases and boarded a train bound for Leadville.

It wasn't long before Maggie met James Joseph Brown. She had always dreamed of marrying a rich man. J.J. Brown wasn't rich, but he was bright, determined and "had promise." He was an aspiring superintendent of the Louisville Mine, while Maggie was a sales clerk at the emporium of Daniels, Fisher and Smith. On September 2, 1886, at age 19, Margaret Tobin married J.J. Brown. The wedding was held at the distinctive Church of the Annunciation on the corner of East 7th and Poplar Streets. A church that had been constructed a few years earlier as a result of the effective fund raising of Father Henry Robinson.

While the silver crash of 1893 depleted the fortunes of many, it was gold and the genius of James Joseph Brown that kept the mining district going. The Little Jonny Mine is centrally located in an area called the Gold Belt, which is located east of Adelaide. The mine, which was a large producer of silver, was the property of John Campion. It was part of the Ibex Mining Company, and was destined to become a huge producer of gold. Campion hired J.J. Brown as superintendent of the Ibex properties in 1893. Brown immediately faced a dilemma. The owners were not able to prevent cave-ins due to the dolomite sand. Brown devised a method to tunnel through the sand, and tapped vast quantities of high-grade gold. His ingenuity was rewarded with 12,500 shares of stock. Production in 1894 was so high that the company paid dividends of $1,000,000. J.J. and Maggie were rich.

James Joseph Brown. *Colorado Pioneer Collection.*

Margaret Tobin Brown, a survivor of the Titanic, became immortalized as "The Unsinkable Molly Brown." *Colorado Pioneer Collection.*

J.J., Maggie, and their two children Lawrence and Helen moved to their new Denver mansion at 1340 Pennsylvania Street, on prestigious Capitol Hill. Molly, as she had become known to Denverites, moved in the circles of Denver society but could not crack the elite Sacred 36. The small exclusive group simply thought that Mrs. Brown lacked an element of refinement and culture. Over the next several years Molly became a world traveler, social climber, philanthropist, heroine, and even had aspirations for political office. Her jewels and elegant wardrobe were as fine as money could buy. She hobnobbed with nobility. Molly learned to speak several languages and traveled with the international set. Following one of her voyages home from Europe in 1912, she became an international celebrity.

Molly Brown booked passage from Cherbourg to New York on the maiden voyage of the Titanic. Nearly five days into the voyage, the ship that was thought to be unsinkable, struck an iceberg. Slowly, in the cold of the night, the great Titanic began sinking into the sea. The passengers and crew totaled 2,228. Less than one-third survived. Molly Brown escaped the catastrophe in lifeboat number six.

Molly loved to embellish the truth, and it certainly helped as she took on the roll of heroine. She stated, "It is true that I was at the oars for five hours, but really, why call me a heroine? I believe that whatever we do is more or less selfish. I rowed to keep away from the suction when the Titanic went down; I rowed to reach the boat whose light we saw later; I rowed to reach the Carpathia. You see it was selfish, wasn't it?" Her expensive Chinchilla coat covered three children, while she joked, and sang songs to keep her boatload of survivors awake and active in the cold of night. Once aboard the rescue ship, she spent her time caring for the injured survivors.

Upon her arrival back in Denver, Molly was quickly accepted into the exclusive Sacred 36. Now a woman of international stature, the society that once shunned her, now welcomed her with open arms.

Molly loved to talk, and now the world was listening. When asked how she accomplished what she did, her reply was, "Typical Brown luck. I'm unsinkable." A legend was born. Years after her death in 1932, Margaret Tobin Brown was assured immortality when her life story was portrayed on stage and screen in *The Unsinkable Molly Brown.*

Although it was the genius of J.J. Brown that made John F. Campion and the other Ibex owners, including himself, ultra rich, he will always be most remembered as the husband of Molly Brown.

The Great Ice Palace

Leadville was dealt a crippling blow in 1893 when President Grover Cleveland repealed the Sherman Silver Purchase Act whereby the government would no longer purchase silver to back its currency. The foreign market for silver collapsed as well. The economy of Leadville rebounded magnificently, however, due in large part to the gold mining success of the Little Jonny. Silver production also eventually bounced back. In 1895, silver production exceeded every year of Leadville's short history with the exception of the boom year of 1880. The total production of area mines was also the greatest since 1889. Money was flowing once more.

Seeking to bring tourists and new money into the community, several businessmen decided to create a new and different attraction – an ice palace. Actually, the idea was not created by Leadville. Montreal and St. Paul had built similar structures. Leadville had talked about doing the same thing for some time, when suddenly the time seemed right. Much went into planning and design. Leadville wanted to build the finest such structure ever constructed. Finally, the design was complete and construction commenced.

Huge blocks of ice were cut from the area's ponds and

The Ice Palace was an extraordinary undertaking, but it didn't last long. *Colorado Historical Society.*

lakes. Some ice even arrived by rail. As many as 250 men were hired to cut the ice and build the palace which covered three acres of a five-acre site. The structure, which looked much like a medieval castle, was constructed with 5,000 tons of ice. There were towers ranging from 60 to 90 feet in height. Within the confines of the five-foot thick walls, was a skating rink which was 80 feet wide by 190 feet long, a grand ballroom, and a large dining room.

The palace officially opened on January 3, 1896, amid much fanfare. City politicians, civic clubs, 2,000 members of the Miners' Union, the Dodge City Cowboy Band and others participated in a huge parade to commemorate the occasion. It was necessary for each of the three railroads serving Leadville to add extra passenger cars to scheduled trains in order to accommodate the throngs of tourists flocking to see the unique structure.

Visitors saw skating exhibitions, or could skate themselves. There was dancing and fine dining. Contests were held and awards given for ice sculpting, skating, dancing, rock drilling, and for costumes.

It was fun while it lasted, but it didn't last long. The winter of 1896 was unusually mild, and the ice began to melt prematurely. The uniqueness of the structure began to wear on both tourists and locals alike. The residents of Leadville grew tired of all the parties and festivities. The structure ultimately became a financial failure. On March 28, 1896, the Ice Palace closed permanently.

Climax Molybdenum

Molybdenite was discovered near Leadville, on Mount Bartlett, close to Fremont Pass in 1879 by prospector Charles Senter. Senter, however, had no idea what he had discovered. It wasn't until 1895 that his mineral was identified as Molybdenite, initially it was the only known ore of Molybdenum. At the time, the metal had no known use. The world's largest deposit of Molybdenite occurs at Climax, Colorado, just 13 miles north of the Cloud City.

During the early 1900s, metallurgists in Germany and France uncovered the great value of Molybdenum. They found that by adding small amounts of the metal to steel, the durability and toughness of the product was greatly increased. World War I revealed the superiority of German guns and armor because they were constructed of Molybdenum alloy steel. Suddenly there was a demand for Molybdenum.

Climax, as it looked prior to their moving several hundred houses to Leadville. *The Climax Mine.*

Basically, the element is used in the process of hardening steel. As an alloying agent, it increases the hardenability of quenched and tempered steels. It also increases the strength of steel at high temperatures. Coatings of molybdenum adhere firmly to metals such as steel, iron and aluminum, to provide an excellent resistance to wear. The most important mineral source and the most common ore of the element is molybdenite, a black platy disulfide.

The Climax Molybdenum Company was organized by Max Schott, and the American Metal Company, in 1917. Production began in 1918 and Moly was stockpiled. When the war ended in November of that year the market collapsed and the Climax Mine was closed in 1919. Like most mining properties, Climax opened and closed as production fluctuated with supply and demand. Brainerd Phillipson, president of Climax Molybdenum, embarked on a massive advertising campaign to convince industry of the peacetime advantages of Molybdenum steel alloys. In 1924, the Climax Mine reopened. Construction of the new Phillipson Tunnel in 1929 increased production, and the Climax Mine began to show a profit. By 1935, all of the company's indebtedness had been paid off, the following year Climax decided to build a company town for its employees, and before long the community had over 1,000 residents. By 1950, the population had grown to 1,600 residents in the town that was North America's highest (11,450 ft.). Later in order to begin open-pit mining where the town existed, Climax decided to relocate its buildings to Leadville. In 1960, 370 houses and three apartment buildings, were moved to a subdivision later to be called West Park.

Molybdenum became a top priority during World War II, and the Climax Mine ran at 150% of its production design capacity during the war years. Production boomed again during the Korean War.

In 1957, the American Metal Company (which had previously owned 25% of the Climax Molybdenum Company) merged with the latter to form a new enterprise known as AMAX, Inc.

By 1962, AMAX was mining 40% of Colorado's mineral production, or approximately 36,000 tons of ore per day. During its highest period of production Climax employed close to 3,000 workers, and paid them well. Lake County had the highest per capita income in Colorado.

Beside the highway on State Route 91, north of Fremont Pass, stands a monument which reads: "In this valley the towns of Robinson, Kokomo and Recen existed. Kokomo was the site of the highest Masonic Lodge in the U.S.A. – Elevation 10,618 feet." The three mining towns, once a part of the Ten-Mile Mining District, were buried forever (in 1971) at the bottom of a tailing pond of the Climax Molybdenum Company. Kokomo was the largest of the three towns. Its post office was established on May 5, 1879. Less than a month later, the town was incorporated and became, at the time, the highest incorporated town in Colorado. Two events that once occurred on present day Climax property, are of interest.

George B. Robinson, for whom the town of Robinson was named, was involved in a dispute regarding the ownership of the Smuggler Mine. Robinson was immensely rich and extremely popular, and had been elected Lieutenant Governor of Colorado in November of 1880. Within a month he died tragically. Expecting violence at the Smuggler, Robinson posted armed guards at the site. On the night of November 27, 1880 he went to the mine to check on his guards. Thinking he was an intruder, one of the guards shot Robinson. He died two days later.

After robbing the Denver Hotel in Breckenridge during the summer of 1898, the notorious Pug Ryan and his gang fled to a cabin near Kokomo. They were tracked down. In the bloody gunfight that followed, two lawmen and two members of Ryan's gang were killed. Ryan escaped, however. Ten years after the robbery, a group of school children found part of the loot stashed in a hollow log near the cabin that was used as a hideout.

By the early 1980s, the Climax operation was moving ore at a record pace, and their stockpiled reserve reached new heights. Once again, it was a matter of supply and demand. The surplus greatly exceeded the demand on the molybdenum market. By 1985 over 2,000 workers had been laid off. Eventually, the Climax Molybdenum Company, ceased doing business. The economy of Leadville, which had relied heavily on the Climax operation, suffered accordingly.

In 1993, Cyprus AMAX Minerals was created through the merger of Cyprus Minerals and AMAX, and the Climax operation became a part of the newly created Cyprus Climax Metals Company. In 1999 the Phelps Dodge Corporation took over the Climax Mine and its sister property the Henderson Mine in Clear Creek County, while the Henderson Mine was still operating. Freeport-McMoRan Copper & Gold, Inc. (FCX) acquired Phelps Dodge in March of 2007 for approximately 25.9 billion dollars in cash and stock. The Climax Mine will undoubtedly bounce back under the direction of FCX.

    Throughout its history, Leadville has seen the boom and bust scenario, over and over, and continued to endure. The proud people of the Cloud City have always held their heads high. Recently, Leadville rebounded nicely from the last Climax closing due predominately to increased tourism. More and more people are learning about this unique city. Leadville is a special place with a special history.

Glossary of Mining Terms

ALLUVIAL DEPOSIT: Sediment deposited by a stream.

ARASTRA: An old Spanish apparatus used to break up ore by means of a heavy stone dragged around a circular trough.

ASSAY: To test and examine ores and minerals by a chemical process or the blowpipe method. Sometimes the assaying process requires the separation of precious metals from base metals by use of a cupel.

BAR: The peripheral accumulation of rocks along the banks of a stream, often worked for gold by prospectors.

CARBONATES: Those ores containing a large amount of carbonate of lead.

CLAIM: A mining claim is the right, or claim, of an individual or company to a specific location with set boundaries, and recorded according to law. Mining laws consider a claim legitimate if sufficient quantities of a metallic or other substance are found rendering the land valuable. Deposits of certain minerals, such as coal and oil, are the property of the United States and are not subject to claim under United States mining laws.

CONCENTRATION: The process by which nonessential and less valuable portions of ore are removed by mechanical means.

CRADLE: See Rocker.

CRIBBING: The process of constructing close timber, such as bulkheading or lining of a shaft.

CROSSCUT TUNNEL: A transverse tunnel which intersects a main tunnel, or drift, at an angle and leads to another point.

CUPEL: A small porous cup used in the assaying process of separate precious metals from lead and other base metals.

DREDGE: Bucket dredges and traction dredges are operated by power and usually are mounted on a boat. The bucket operates like an elevator and brings continuous loads of sand and gravel to the deck where it passes through the sluice. Traction dredges scoop much in the manner of a steam shovel. Suction dredges are smaller and often portable.

DRIFT: An underground tunnel which follows a vein. Usually the mine's main tunnel.

FISSURE VEIN: A crack in the earth's surface rock which is filled with a mineral matter other than that of its surrounding walls.

FLOAT: Pieces of ore which have washed away or have fallen from their parent veins. The discovery of float was usually the catalyst to trace each fragment toward its source.

GELENA: A common lead sulphide which often has silver content.

HYDRAULIC MINING: High pressure water is carried through a hose and nozzle and used to wash away gold bearing earth. The water and earth are carried through sluices which separate the gold.

IRON PYRITE: A mineral which resembles gold. Commonly called "fool's gold".

LODE: A vein or tabular deposit of precious mineral.

LONG TOM: A device used in the early mining days to aid in the separation of materials. Gravel is shoveled into the long tom, through which water is funneled, and worked with a hoe or rake. Gold and other heavier minerals are then swept through a screen and caught in the riffles beyond.

MILL: An establishment in which ores are reduced by means other than smelting.

MINE: Technically it is an ore deposit – a rich or abundant source. Commonly considered the pit, excavation, or tunnel from which ores and precious minerals, etc. are taken from the earth.

MINING DISTRICT: An area of country usually located within certain natural boundaries, and designated by name, in which a substantial amount of mining activity occurs.

MOTHER LODE: The predominant vein, or lode, passing through a particular area. Prospectors dreamed of discovering a mother lode.

NUGGET: A lump of native precious metal (i.e. a gold nugget).

ORE DEPOSIT: The primary source of the mineral which occurs in a vein.

PAN: The slowest method in searching for gold is panning. Water is swirled in a circular motion over the earth and gravel in a flat shallow pan. Sand and earth are gradually washed away.

PLACER MINING: Surface deposit mining, as placer mining is sometimes called, is one of the oldest methods. Water action has already extracted the precious material and deposited it in more accessible places to be worked, such as stream beds, etc.

QUARTZ: A common opaque mineral sometimes found near richer deposits.

REDUCTION WORKS: Any plant which reduces metal from its ore (i.e. a smelting works).

RIFFLE: The bottom of a sluice or trough with slats spaced closely together in order to catch gold and other heavy minerals.

ROCKER: An early mining device, sometimes called a cradle. Earth and gravel are shoveled into a sieve box in the top of the rocker. Water is channeled over the sieve as the device is rocked to and fro. Heavier gold filters to a trough where it is caught by the riffles.

SAMPLING WORKS: An establishment in which ores are sampled to determine their value.

SLUICE: In areas where their was a good water supply, the sluice was one of the most popular devices used by miners. Dirt is shoveled into the long trough with transverse riffles. The water flow washes away waste material leaving gold and other heavy materials in the riffles.

SMELTING: A process by which metals are reduced from their ores by fusion, in a furnace or crucible.

STAMP MILL: An establishment or works where rock is crushed by steam-powered or water-powered pestles or stamps (i.e. a quartz mill).

TAILINGS: Residue which is left behind after precious metals have been separated from the ore by concentration or dressing.

TELLURIDE: A rich ore containing compounds of tellurium and gold and/or silver.

TRAMWAY: A cable system, suspended between two points, by which ore or other material may be transported by buckets.

VEIN: An elongated mineral deposit, or fissure, often rich in content.

VUG: An open cavity in a rock or formation which is sometimes lined with crystalline deposits.

WILFLEY TABLE: A table used in ore dressing for concentrating and separating various metals. A jerking motion allows light grains to wash over a riffled surface while heavy grains remain. An important Colorado invention which increased recovery and profits.

WIRE GOLD OR SILVER: Native gold or silver in a maze of wire-like threads.

> Visit the National Mining Hall of Fame and Museum at:
> 120 West Ninth Street in Leadville, Colorado.

Bibliography

BOOKS

Bancroft, Caroline. *Augusta Tabor: Her Side of the Scandal.* Boulder: Johnson Publishing Co., 1955.

Bancroft, Caroline. *Silver Queen: The Fabulous Story of Baby Doe Tabor.* Boulder: Johnson Publishing Co., 1955.

Bancroft, Caroline. *Six Racy Madams of Colorado.* Boulder: Johnson Publishing Co., 1965.

Bancroft, Caroline. *Tabor's Matchless Mine and Lusty Leadville.* Boulder: Johnson Publishing Co., 1960.

Bateman, Alan M. *Economic Mineral Deposits.* New York: John Wiley and Sons, Inc., 1958.

Blair, Edward. *Everybody Came to Leadville.* Leadville: Timberline Books, 1971.

Blair, Edward. *Leadville: Colorado's Magic City.* Boulder: Pruett Publishing Co., 1980.

Bueler, Gladys R. *Colorado's Colorful Characters.* Boulder: Pruett Publishing Co., 1981.

Burke, John. *The Legend of Baby Doe, The Life and Times of the Silver Queen of the West.* Lincoln: University of Nebraska Press, 1974.

Coquoz, Rene. *A Century of Medicine in Leadville, Colorado, 1860-1960.* Leadville: Rene L. Coquoz Books, 1967.

Coquoz, Rene. *Tales of Early Leadville.* Leadville: Rene L. Coquoz Books, 1966.

Crofutt, George A. *Crofutt's Grip-Sack Guide of Colorado.* Boulder: Johnson Books, 1885.

Dawson, John Frank. *Place Names In Colorado.* Denver: J. F. Dawson Publishing Co., 1954.

Dill, R.G. *History of the Arkansas Valley, Colorado.* Chicago: Baskin and Co., 1881.

Dyer, J.L. *Snow-shoe Itinerant.* Cincinnati: Cranston & Stowe, 1890. Reprinted Breckenridge: Father Dyer United Methodist Church, 1975.

Fay, Abbott. *Famous Coloradans.* Ronia: Mountaintop Books, 1990.

Fossett, Frank. *Colorado.* New York: C.G. Crawford, 1880.

George, R.D. *Colorado Geological Survey.* Denver: The Smith-Brooks Printing Co., 1909.

Gandy, Lewis Cass. *The Tabors.* New York: The Press of the Pioneers, Inc., 1934.

Griswold, Don L. and Jean W. Griswold. *History of Leadville and Lake County: From Mountain Solitude to Metropolis.* Niwot: Colorado Historical Society/University of Colorado Press, 1996.

Griswold, Don L. and Jean W. Griswold. *The Carbonate Camp Called Leadville*. Denver: University of Denver, 1951.

Hall, Frank. *History of the State of Colorado*. 4 Vols. Chicago: Blakely Printing Co., 1889, 1890, 1891, 1895.

Hollister, Ovando J. *The Mines of Colorado*. Springfield, MA: Samuel Bowles & Company, 1867.

Lamm, Richard D. and Duane A. Smith. *Pioneers and Politicians*. Boulder: Pruett Publishing Company, 1984.

Larsh, Ed B. and Robert Nichols. *Leadville U. S. A.* Boulder: Johnson Books, 1993.

May, Stephen. *Pilgrimage: A Journey Through Colorado's History and Culture*. Athens, OH: Swallow Press, 1987.

Monnett, John H. *Colorado Profiles: Men and Women Who Shaped the Centennial State*. Evergreen: Cordillera Press, 1987.

Noel, Thomas J. *Historical Atlas of Colorado*. Norman: University of Oklahoma Press, 1993.

Poor, M.C. *Denver, South Park & Pacific*. Denver: Rocky Mountain Railroad Club, 1976.

Pough, Frederick H. *A Field Guide to Rocks and Minerals*. Boston: Houghton Mifflin Company, 1955.

Rinehart, Frederick R. *Chronicles of Colorado*. Boulder: Roberts Rinehart, Inc., 1984.

Schulze, Suzanne (Ed.). *A Century of the Colorado Census*. Greeley: University of Northern Colorado, 1976.

Skala, Helen and Dora Krocesky. *Leadville's Tales From the Old Timers*. Leadville: Skala and Krocesky, 1972.

Skala, Helen. *Leadville's Tales From the Old Timers: Book 2*. Leadville: Skala, 1977.

Smith, Duane A. *Horace Tabor: His Life and Legend*. Boulder: University of Colorado Press, 1989.

Ubbelohde, Carl. *A Colorado History*. Boulder: Pruett Press, Inc., 1965.

Voynick, Stephen M. *Climax: The History of Colorado's Climax Molybdenum Mine*. Missoula: Mountain Press, 1996.

Voynick, Stephen M. *Leadville, a Miner's Epic*. Missoula: Mountain Press, 1986.

Voynick, Stephen M. *The Making of a Hardrock Miner*. Berkeley: Howell-North, 1978.

Wolle, Muriel Sibell. *Stampede to Timberline*. Denver: Sage Books, 1962.

NEWSPAPERS

Carbonate Chronicle (Leadville)
Denver Post
Evening News - Dispatch (Leadville)
Fairplay Flume
Herald Democrat (Leadville)
Leadville Chronicle
Leadville Daily Herald
Park County Republican
Rocky Mountain News

ARTICLES

Halaas, David Fridtjof and Gerald C. Morton. "Boom and Bust: Images from the Colorado Chronicle." Colorado Heritage. Colorado Historical Society. (Issues 1 & 2, 1983).

Harvey, Mrs. James R. "The Leadville Ice Palace of 1896." Colorado Magazine 17, No. 3. (May, 1940): 94-101.

Smith, Duane A. and David Fridtjof Halaas. "A Fifty-Niner Miner: The Career of Horace W. Tabor." Colorado Heritage. Colorado Historical Society. (Issues 1 & 2, 1983).

Voynick, Stephen M. "Climax Molybdenum: One of the World's Great Mines." Mining Engineering (September 1997).

MAPS & CHARTS

Map of Colorado Territory, Embracing the Central Gold Region. Drawn by Frederick J. Ebert under direction of the Governor, Wm. Gilpin. Published by Jacob Monk, 1862.

Map of the Consolidated Ten Mile Mining District. By Max Boehmer and Victor G. Hills, 1881.

Map of Public Surveys in Colorado Territory. To accompany report of the Surveyor General, 1866, (Issued by the General Land Office on Oct. 2, 1866.)

Map of the State of Colorado, 1885. Compiled from the Official Records of the General Land Office, Compiled and drawn by M. Hendges.

Nell's New Topographical and Township Map of the State of Colorado. Compiled from U.S. Government Surveys and other authentic Sources, 1881.

Nell's Map of Colorado, 1885. Chain and Hardy Co., Agent, Denver, 1885.

Technical Information, Climax Molybdenum Company. Printed by AMAX, Inc. (undated)

Thayer's Map of Colorado, Published by H. L. Thayer, Denver, 1880. From Surveys of the General Land Office, used by permission, revised and corrected to date by the Publisher.

United States Geological Survey, Maps, U.S. Department of the Interior, Federal Center, Denver.

OTHER SOURCES

Encyclopedia of American Business History and Biography: Railroads of the Nineteenth Century. New York: Bruccoli Clark Layman, Inc., 1988.

First Annual Colorado Mining Directory, 1896. Compiled by J.S. Bartow and P.A. Simmons. Denver: The Colorado Mining Directory Co. Leadville City Directories, Archives, University of Colorado at Boulder.

Leadville Mining District compiled from official records and other reliable sources, January 1901. Charles F. Saunders. Also copyright 1901 by Charles F. Saunders.

McKenney's Business Directory of Principal Towns in California, Nevada, Utah, Wyoming, Colorado and Nebraska 1882. San Francisco: H.S. Crocker & Co., Publishers, 1882.

Technical Information. Climax Molybdenum Company, Climax, Colorado. (Undated)

This is Climax Molybdenum. Climax Molybdenum Company, AMAX, Inc., 1979. Underlying Value, Freeport - McMoRan Copper & Gold, Inc., Annual Report, 2006.

U.S. Bureau of the Census, Revised by the Social Science Research Council. The Statistical History of the United States from Colonial Times to the Present. Stanford: Fairfield Publishers, Inc., 1965.

Index

A

Adelaide 85
Adelaide Mine, the 61
Allen, Billy 58, 59
AMAX, Inc 92
American Metal Company, the 92
American Smelting & Refining Company, the 63
Amity Mine, the 66
Amstead, Kate 56
Anson, John 69, 70
Anthony, Susan B. 43
Arkansas Valley Plant 63
Arvada, Colorado 7
Aspen, Colorado 64, 66
Arthur, Chester (President) 35
A.Y. Mine, the 41

B

Bank of Leadville, the 27, 28, 46
Barrett, Laurence 41
Bella Union, the 49
Bernhardt, Sarah 41
Billing and Eilers Smelter, the 63
Billy Nye's Saloon 50
Black Hawk 31, 32
Black Prince Mine, the 61
Bloodsworth, James M. 50
Bockhaus, Carl 52, 53
Boettcher, Charles 42
Bon Ton, the 49
Borden, John 25
Boulder Mine, the 62
Breece Hill 47
Broken Nose Scotty 47
Brown, James Joseph "J. J." 85 - 88
Brown Palace Hotel, the 37
Brown, "The Unsinkable" Molly 85 - 88
Brumley, Colorado 65, 66
Bucket of Blood, the 49
Buckskin Joe, Colorado 9, 22, 24

Bucktown 62, 63
Buena Vista, Colorado 81
Buffalo Bill's Wild West Show 43
Bull's Eye Mine, the 16
Burnell, Joseph 42
Bush, Bill 37

C

Cache Creek 69
California Gulch 13, 14, 21, 22, 24, 25, 43, 55, 63
Camp Hale 68
Campion, John F. 42, 61, 65, 67, 85, 88
Carbonate Chronicle 19
Carbonate Concert Hall, the 49
Carbonate National Bank 44
Carpathia, the 87
Carpenter, Cass 16
Chaffee, Jerome B. 26, 27, 28
Chestnut Street 17, 51
Chicken Hill 68
Chrysolite Mine, the 27, 83
Church of the Annunciation 85
City Hotel, the 25
Clanton, Ike 58
Clarendon Hotel, the 32, 33, 36, 41, 81
Cleveland, Grover (President) 35, 89
Climax, Colorado 91
Climax Mine, the 91, 92, 94
Climax Molybdenum Company, the 92, 93, 104, 105
Cody, William F. "Buffalo Bill" (Colonel) 43
Colorado Central Railroad, the 66
Colorado Edison Telephone Company, the 28
Colorado Midland Railroad, the 81
Colorado Prince Mine, the 62
Cook, David J. 83
Coon Row 49, 56, 68
Corbett, James 41
Coronado Mine, the 84
Cyprus AMAX Minerals 93
Cyprus Climax Metals Company 93

D

Daniels, W. B. 42
Delaware Hotel, the 19
Denver and South Park Stage Line 79
Denver, Colorado 7, 8, 33 - 38, 42, 57, 67, 82, 83, 87

Denver & Rio Grande Railroad, the 79
Denver, South Park and Pacific Railroad, the 80, 81
Denver Times, the 38
Deuel, Maude 49
DeWalt, Frank W. 46
Dexter, James Viola 42
Doe, Elizabeth McCourt *See* Tabor, Elizabeth McCourt "Baby Doe"
Doe, W. H. Sr. (Colonel) 31
Doe, William Harvey Jr. 31, 32
Dougan, Dr. David H. 44
Duggan, Martin 50 - 52, 54, 55
Durango, Colorado 34
Dyer, Father John 43

E

Eclipse Mine, the 36
Elder, Kate (Mary Katherine Haroney) 59
Elkins, John 52
Eureka Mine, the 61
Evans, Laura 43
Everett, Colorado 65
Everett, C. M. 65, 66
Evergreen Lakes 76

F

Fairplay, Colorado 9, 47
Father Struck It Rich 67
Favorite Mine, the 62
Fenton, James 44
Field, Marshall 42
Finntown 61, 68
Foley, Tim 28
Freeport-McMoRan Copper & Gold, Inc. (FCX) 94
Fremont Pass 91, 93
French Row 49
Frodsham, Edward 53
Fryer, George H. 24 - 27, 43
Fryer Hill 24 - 27
Fulford, Arthur H. 71
Fulford, Colorado 71, 72

G

Glenwood Springs, Colorado 59
Goodell, Annie 75
Goodell, Clara 75

Goodell, Jennie 75
Goodell, Mary 75
Goodell, Olive 75
Goodell, Roswell Eaton 75
Grand Central Theatre, the 51
Granite, Colorado 69
Grant, James Benton 76
Grant Smelter, the 76
Grant, Ulysses S. (President) 9, 76, 81
Great Northern Hotel, the 63
Great Western Auction House and Clothing Store, the 42
Greeley, Horace 7
Griffin Mine, the 66
Guggenheim, Meyer 41
Gunfight at the O.K. Corral 57

H

Halfway House, the 65
Haroney, Mary Katherine *See* Elder, Kate
Harris, George Albert 25
Harrison Avenue 16, 18, 19, 32, 49, 54, 68, 73, 74
Harrison, Edwin 16
Harrison, T. H. 50, 51
Hastings, Heon 69, 70
Hayes, Rutherford B. (President) 9
Healy House Museum 42
Henderson, George L. 25
Henderson Mine, the 94
Herald Democrat 19
Higgenbottom, Joseph "Buckskin Joe" 22
Hines, Charlie 52
Holliday, John Henry "Doc" 57, 58, 59
Homestake Peak 46
Hook, George 26
Hotel Windsor, the 74
Houdini, Harry 41
Humboldt Mine, the 61
Hyman's Saloon 58

I

Ibex Mines 61
Ibex Mining Company 61, 85
Ice Palace, the 89, 90
Independence Pass 64 - 66
Inter-Laken Hotel, the 65, 66
Iron Hill 16

Iron Mask Mine, the 42
Iron Mine, the 16

J

Jackson, George 7
Jacktown 62, 68
Jeffrey, Robert 70
John Philip Sousa's Marine Band 41
Jones, Marc 69, 70
Jones, William 56
Joyce, Milt 57, 58

K

Kelly, P. A. 52
King, George E. 19
Kokomo, Colorado 93

L

Lake County Bank 27
Lake, Pastor Arthur 43
Lamb, Lewis 54, 55, 56
Lamb, Mindy 55, 56
Langrishe, Jack 41, 54
Lavery, Tom 51
Leadville Athletic Association 77
Leadville Blues, the 77
Leadville Daily Herald 19
Leadville Democrat 19
Leadville Dispatch 19
Leadville Fire Department, the 73
Leadville Hose Company No. 2 84
Leadville Star 19
Lee, Abe 13, 21, 22
Lime Mine, the 16
Little Bob Mine, the 62
Little Casino, the 49
Little Chicago 62, 63
Little Ellen Mine, the 62
Little Jonny Mine, the 61, 63, 67, 85, 89
Little Pittsburg Consolidated Mining Company 26
Little Pittsburg Mine, the 26, - 28
Little Stray Horse Gulch 61
Lode, Gregory 7
Londoner, Wolfe 23
Louise Mine, the 62

Louisville Mine, the 85
Lovell, "Chicken Bill" 27

M

Machebeuf, Father Joseph P. 43
Maid of Erin Mine, the 43
Malta, Colorado 25, 28, 63, 64
Masterson, William Barclay "Bat" 79, 80
Matchless Mine, the 28, 36, 38, 39
Mater, Charles 24
May Company, the 42
May, David 42, 43
May, Madame Mollie 49, 56
McClelland, William 79
McCombe, Jack 43
McCourt, Peter 37
McIntire, Albert W. (Governor) 84
McLain, Edward B. 67
McLain, Evalyn Walsh 67
Merchants' Protective Patrol, the 52
Meyer, August R. 16
Miner Boy Mine, the 62
Miners Exchange, the 27
Moffat, David H. 26 - 28
Mooney, Michael 83
Moore, A. P. 28
Morlacchi, Mademoiselle Guiseppina 43
Morning Glory Mine, the 61
Morning Star Mine, the 42
Morrisey, John D. 45, 46
Mosquito Pass 9, 22, 44
Mosquito Range 9, 43, 47
Mountain Boy Gulch 65
Mount Bartlett 91
Mount Campion 65
Mt. Elbert 64
Mt. Silverheels 24
Mullen, Charles J. 14

N

National, the 49
New Discovery, the 26, 27
Nott, Silas W. 79
Nye, Billy 25, 50

O

O'Connor, George 50
Odeon, the 49
O'Donovan Rossa, the 45
Ollie Reed Mine, the 62
Omohundro, John B. "Texas Jack" 42, 43
Oriental Saloon, the 57
Oro City 13, 14, 22, 24, 25, 55, 61, 63, 69
Oro Mining Ditch and Fluming Company 14, 16

P

Pacific House Hotel, the 22
Palmer, William (General) 80
Paul, J. Marshal 14
Pawnee Indians 43
Phelps Dodge Corporation, the 94
Phillipson, Brainerd 92
Phillipson Tunnel, the 92
Pike, Zebulon Montgomery 7
Pioneer Ladies' Aid Society, the 35
Pioneer, the 49
Pitkin, Frederick R. (Governor) 83
Platte Canyon 80
President Mine, the 66
Pride, Madame Mollie 49
Printer Boy Mine, the 14, 24
Pueblo, Colorado 79, 80
Purdy, Madame Winnie 46, 54, 56
Purple, Madame Sallie 49, 56

R

Ralston, Lewis 7
Recen, Colorado 93
Red Light Hall 49
Red Stockings 55, 56
Rische, August 25 - 27
Robert Emmet Mine, the 84
Robinson, Colorado 93
Robinson, Father Henry 43, 85
Robinson, George B. 93
Robitaille, Eugene 19
Rock Hill 16
Rock Mine, the 16
Rocky Mountain News 22
Rogers, Buck 71, 72
Routt, John L. (Governor) 25, 42
Royal Gorge 79, 80

Ruby Mine, the 66
Russell, William Green 7
Ryan House, the 64
Ryan, Pug 93

S

Saddle Rock Café 32
Saint George's Episcopal Church 76
Saint Kevins, Colorado 46, 66, 67
Saint Kevins Mine, the 66
Sandelowsky, Jake. *See* Sands, Jake
Sands, Jake 32, 33
Santa Fe Railroad, the 79
Schott, Max 92
Senter, Charles 91
Sherman Silver Purchase Act 35, 89
Shoo-Fly 32
Silverheels 22 - 24
Slate Mountain 71
Smelter Valley 62, 65
Smith, Cooper 14
Smith, Jefferson Randolph "Soapy Smith" 56, 57
Smuggler, the 93
Soda Springs 76
South Park 22, 24, 79 - 81
South Paw Mine, the 70, 71
Spotswood, Robert W. 79
Star Mountain 65
Star of Blood 38
State Street 43, 49, 50, 52, 56, 67
Stein, Orth Harper 46
Stevens, William H. 14
Stewart, Patrick 52, 54
St. George's Episcopal Church 19
Stillborn Alley 49
St. Louis Mine, the 16, 62
St. Louis Smelting and Refining Company 16
Stone Mine, the 16
Stratton, Winfield Scott 36
Stray Horse Gulch 61, 62, 68
Stringtown 62 - 64
Stumptown 61, 62
Sugar Loaf Mountain 69
Sullivan, John L. 41
Swilltown 63
Swilltown Smelter, the 63

T

Tabor Block, the 36
Tabor, Elizabeth Bonduel Lillie 34, 35, 37
Tabor, Elizabeth McCourt "Baby Doe" 29, 31 - 39
Tabor Grand Hotel, the 16, 19
Tabor Grand Opera House 34
Tabor, Horace Austin Warner "H. A. W." 7, 19, 21, 22, 24 - 29, 32 - 37, 39, 41, 51, 83
Tabor Light Cavalry, the 83
Tabor, Louisa Augusta Pierce 21, 22, 24, 29, 33 - 35, 37
Tabor, Nathaniel Maxcy 22, 36, 37
Tabor, Rose Mary Echo Silver Dollar 34, 35, 37, 38
Teller, Henry 35
10th Mountain Division, U. S. Army 68
Texas House, the 49, 55
Thompson, Ben 79
Tiger Alley 49
Tilden, Samuel 9
Tintown 63
Titanic, the 86, 87
Tobin, Margaret "Maggie" *See* Brown, "The Unsinkable" Molly
Tombstone, Arizona 57, 58
Tontine Restaurant, the 51
Turquoise Lake 66
Twin Lakes, Colorado 46, 64 - 66, 76
Tyler, Johnny 57, 58

U

Union Pacific Railroad 81
Unsinkable Molly Brown, the 86, 88
Updegraff, Louise H. 44
Uzzell, Reverend Tom A. 43, 47, 48

V

Van Brooklyn, William 24
Vendome Hotel, the *See* Tabor Grand Hotel
Vestal, Madame 43

W

Walsh, Thomas 66, 67
Wanklin, Price 44
Watson, Edmund "Ed" 53, 54

West Chestnut Street 51
Western Federation of Miners, the 83, 84
Weston Pass 47
Wilde, Oscar 41
Wilgas, T. B. 28
Winnie Mine, the 62
Wood, Alvinus B. 14
Wyman, Pop 15

Y

Youngson, Bailey 55

OTHER WORKS BY DAVE SOUTHWORTH

BOOKS: NON-FICTION
Famous Gunfights of the American West
Famous Gunfights of Texas
Feuds on the Western Frontier
Colorado Gold Dust: Short Stories and Profiles
Ghost Towns and Mining Camps of the San Juans
Colorado Mining Camps
Gunfighters of the Old West
Gunfighters of the Old West II

BOOKS: FICTION
Franklin Hall
Rhymes of a Storyteller

VIDEOS
Colorado Mining Camps: A Pictorial Treasure of the Gold and Silver Boom
Leadville: The Boom Years
Mining Camps of the San Juans
Cripple Creek and the Mining Camps of Teller County
The Mining Camps of Northwest Colorado
Boulder County Mining Camps: A Look Back
The Mining Camps of Gilpin and Clear Creek Counties
The Mining Camps of South Central Colorado

AUDIO BOOKS
Colorado Gold Dust: Short Stories and Profiles
Gunfighters of the Old West
Billy the Kid and the Lincoln County War
Jesse James and the James-Younger Gang
Doc Holliday and the Earp Brothers

www.ingramcontent.com/pod-product-compliance
Lightning Source LLC
Chambersburg PA
CBHW071005080526
44587CB00015B/2359